d Rock, Invalid Toffee, Ch…late Crisp
ts Imperial Acids Orange …Ba
Tablets Super Rose Refreshers …ulley
Indian Limes Brandy Balls Super Clove
Raspberry Crystals Footballs Fancy B
ancy Boxes Brompton Tablets Cherry
ch Extra Strong Peppermints Koffades
Sez You Toffee Bobbies Choco Japs
arnival Fruits Clickety Clicks Foaming
ars Big Ben Bars Bo'sun Bars Egg & M
Glider Bars Licorice Flaps Long 'Uns
erry Dab Suckers Treacle Jacks Watta L
s Chesties Boat Race Chews I-Kan-Ch
Snax Winter Lumps Grape Fruit Brick
ingers Colonial Fruits Texas Fruits Bu
ff Kops Dolly Rock Blackcurrant Satin
ts Brandy Kegs Buttermint Tubs Lem
e Bricks North Pole Tablets Winter Sna
Cats Tongues Paradise Plums Phizoggs

THE TREBOR STORY

Matthew Crampton

First published in 2012 by Muddler Books.
www.muddlerbooks.com
© 2012 Matthew Crampton

ISBN 978-0-9561361-1-4

Designed by Matthew Crampton
Set in 11/14pt Garamond
Printed by Henry Ling Limited, Dorchester

Front cover image: Trebor's Forest Gate factory in East London during the 1950s.
Back cover image: striping *Bullseyes* during the 1950s.

www.thetreborstory.com

Image Credits
Most of the images in this book come from the Kraft Foods UK Archives and are reproduced with the permission of Kraft Foods. Trebor, Cadbury and Kraft Foods trademarks, and current Trebor product imagery, are used with the permission of Kraft Foods. I would like to thank the following individuals and organisations for giving permission: Ian and John Marks, various images. London Borough of Newham Arts & Heritage: Rothsay Road (p11), Stratford Viaduct (p12), WW1 ration book (p18), Clarnico staff log (p19), Boleyn Sweets (p25), Snow White packaging (p31), Jubilee Mixture & Gala Mixture (p34), Frollies (p41), Boleyn Tiny Tots (p41), Festival Mixture (p41), bomb damage (p43), Clarnico ad (p82), Clarnico fire brigade (p83), Clarnico workers 1908 (p83), Clarnico petition (p83). David Hale/MAPCO A-Z map (p12). Royal Institute of British Architects: Alexandra Temperance Hotel (p8). Museum of London: Cat's Meat Man (p10). The Olympic Park Legacy Company supplied the image on page 142 and urged me to say 'this image is illustrative only and indicative of the aspirations for the future Park and should be viewed as such. It will be subject to changes as the plans for the Park and area develop over time.'

Contents

Introduction

When I was ten I went away on a weeklong school trip. Into a pocket deep within my little suitcase my mother put fourteen rolls of *Refreshers*, a special stash, two rolls a day, to sustain me through this longest ever separation from family. I still think sometimes of those smooth, sweet cylinders. Back then, the early 1970s, my parents remained keen on rationing: no fizzy drinks, no TV on schooldays except Blue Peter and one treat out of the sweet tin after meals. So imagine my awe at A) being granted two whole rolls of *Refreshers* every day for a week and B) being given them all at once. Now I would have to manage my own rationing.

For many children, sweets are their first brush with conscious desire. Sweets shape their sense of longing. And, let's not forget, sweets deliver. Unlike a lot of things for a child, they provide what they promise. They give the hit. While later, much later, you learn the sluggard cost of that early rush, as a kid this means nothing. All that counts is the hit, the buzz, the fizz, the joy.

No wonder, then, that people revel in remembering their childhood sweets. They relish a rollcall of *Fruit Salad, Woppa Chews, Topps* and *Curly Wurlies*. Those old enough will talk of visits to the sweet shop, the wall of large jars, the tough choices thrust onto tiny shoulders, the twist on the paper bags to contain the delights decanted therein, the lovely lumps those bags formed in your school trouser pockets. Yes, this is nostalgia pure and uncut, but it's also a rekindling of that flame of desire, the lifeforce which adulthood is dedicated to coralling.

But as a child I had a secret up my sleeve. My uncle ran a sweet factory. In fact he ran several sweet factories – and he was the man who made the *Refreshers* and the *Black Jacks* and those huge Sharps Easter Eggs that arrived every Spring. My uncle John was not Willy Wonka, but he might have been. He was John Marks and his grandfather Sydney H Marks was one of the founders of Robertson & Woodcock, which became Trebor. My parents weren't of that family, my mother's sister had married into it, but I had a connection.

This doesn't mean my childhood was flooded with sweets. But I did get to visit the Trebor factory at Woodford in Essex, a glorious day of smells, haircaps and As Many Sweets As I Wanted. I only went there once – even factory visits were rationed – but I always thought I'd go back. And now I have, in a way, as I've written a book about it.

The story starts in 1907 when four bold men set up a small venture to boil sugar and make sweets. They lived in an economic wild west, a young city which had recently arisen on the marshland across the River Lee from the old East End of London. This new East End, around the boroughs of East Ham and West Ham, was ripe turf for plucky venturers. The young firm of Robertson and Woodcock pulled ahead of its many competitors by doing clever things: buying machinery from Germany, ditching horses for motorised delivery vans and grabbing the opportunities of wartime. It expanded constantly, first by building more factory then by acquiring other firms. By the late forties it was a major confectioner. By the seventies it was Britain's biggest maker of sugar sweets. The family of one of its founders, Sydney Marks, steered most of this growth and controlled the firm. Then finally, in 1989, the Marks family sold Trebor to Cadbury. Though the brandname survived, the firm was finished.

As a company, Trebor has good tales to tell. How a mighty business emerges from tiny, uncertain beginnings. How a few ambitious people can shape the lives of many thousands. How its progress, like most progress, is haphazard, leaning on luck as much as guile or industry. How one family manages to keep its business private, and virtuous, even as it totters under the challenges of growth, competition and inner discord.

Beyond these personal stories, Trebor is also a story of Britain's industrial past. Its founders rode a wave of new technology, explored fresh ways of working, and pioneered new sales techniques and export activities. They coped with two world wars. They coped with the ensuing peace. They coped with times of plenty and times of poverty. And when it became hard for a private company to compete with global competitors, they sold the business, as decently as they could and much more decently than they needed.

Such stories are usually nostalgic. This, I'm afraid, is no exception. Back in 1936 Trebor sold 452 different lines. No wonder shopping was slower then; with products like *Harlequin Balls, Rhubarb Custard* and *Raspberry Dab Suckers*, it took ages just to read their names. Today the Trebor brandname has a higher share of the confectionery market than in 1936, but it achieves this with just four products: *Extra Strong Mints, Softmints, Softfruits* and *Extra Strong Mint Gum*. There's little excitement or desire in those names. They're plain, 'does what it says on the tin' sort of names. That is how today's Trebor brand is configured – a no nonsense mint brand designed primarily for adults.

Little surprise, buying sweets is less fun today. The supermarkets that control shopping and the global conglomerates that control food production prefer to limit choice. It's less work for them. So there are fewer names to choose from. And shopping for sweets is less a thoughtful process of selection than an efficient collection of the product pre-selected by our sub-conscious from the branding and marketing to which we've been subjected. Where once you waited for sweets to be weighed out, now you grab them while standing at the till. You don't think, you take.

And the latter story of Trebor the company is, in some ways, a mirror to this limiting of options, this coralling of desire. For where Trebor today is simply a brandname for mostly breath-freshening devices for adults, it was once so much more. No longer are there Trebor factories, Trebor employees, Trebor depots, Trebor sales vans, Trebor newsletters, Trebor works outings, Trebor darts teams or Trebor annual reports. Now Trebor is part of Cadbury, which is itself a bit of the global food behemoth Kraft Foods.

That said, the Marks family did their fair share of acquisition. Trebor bought up other sweet firms like Sharps, Clarnico and Maynards, each with their own heritage, some which still exist as brandnames but none as industrial entities. So in one way there's nothing unusual about Trebor in the economic foodchain: it swallowed some others then got swallowed itself.

But what's lost today are the ideals of family ownership. Without public shareholders to satisfy, the Marks family could make decisions unthinkable today. As late as the 1980s they forbade night shifts at their new Colchester factory so workers might have better family life. They repeatedly reinvested profits rather than harvest them as dividends. And when they sold the company, they hunted down many ex-employees to give them, unbidded, a share of the gain.

As always, it's wise to resist rose-tinted spectacles. The great Sydney J Marks, father to my uncle John and his brother Ian, and the architect of much of Trebor's success, was an autocratic boss. He ran the firm like a fiefdom, with loyal consiglieri to provide advice but few external directors to get in his way. Sydney did not like trade unions and resisted their involvement in Trebor factories. Yet this wasn't simple union-bashing; rather, he didn't want anything to come between him and his beloved employees. As a result, working conditions – and loyalty to staff – were better than in most unionised plants. The despotism was benign.

Moreover, for a family so firmly in control, the Marks were strangely keen on exposing themselves to external scrutiny. They loved consultants. As early as 1936 they invited organisations such as The Institute for Industrial Psychology to probe their workings. Through the sixties and seventies Trebor pioneered management thinking from innovators such as the Tavistock Institute in London. In the 1980s their new Colchester factory gave more responsibility to workers on the production line, and flatter management structures, than most British industry had ever seen: no clocking in, no charge hands and one canteen for all.

This echoed a tradition across the confectionery industry, particularly within Quaker firms like Cadbury, Rowntree and Fry. Quakers try to set every decision within a moral context. They also tend to think long term. Cadbury's Bournville village, started in the 1890s to provide workers with decent housing and community, still sits more sturdily a hundred years later than many developments from the last decade or two. But Cadbury went public in 1962, Rowntree a lot earlier. By the time John and Ian Marks took over from their father Sydney in the 1970s, Trebor was one of few major British firms still under family control.

Just as nature abhors a vacuum, so corporate capitalism negates any perspective beyond profit. It also destroys anyone unwilling to mortgage themselves for growth. As a debt-averse, organically-focused family firm, Trebor could not survive in this new world of titanic global corporations. In 1989 it sold to Cadbury – already far from a family firm and later unable to resist being sucked into Kraft Foods.

If Trebor's four founders were young today, it's unlikely they would be attracted to the confectionery industry. They might rather work in digital media or some other field where there's still scope for enterprise and style. But back in the bustle of Edwardian London, it was an easy, exciting thing to boil some sugar, handwrap some sweets and then hustle them to local shops.

Which is where our story begins…

1907–1918

GETTING STARTED

They never planned an empire. They simply sought a cheaper way to provide local shops with sweets. As the twentieth century dawned across the hungry, rising boroughs of East London, four men pooled their skills and ventured their ambition upon a humble sugar-boiling business.

The founders meet

Thomas King was a wholesaler of food in London's new eastern boroughs. Thinking it might be profitable to branch out into making sweets, he took his friend Robert Robertson to watch a master confectioner at work – a sugar boiler named William Woodcock.

Imagine you could travel back to a sweet factory of the early twentieth century. The first thing you notice is the mess. Strewn across the floor are ashes and sawdust from the coke fire. You walk carefully to avoid slipping on pools of water – or sticking to piles of syrup, spilt onto the floorboards from vast boiling pans. Above, you see rafters coated in starch and dust. It is hot, noisy and filthy, nothing like a modern place for preparing food. The workers wear baggy Edwardian clothes which, along with their voluminous hairstyles (seldom checked by a cap), often brush the sweets they are making. Their aprons are so steeped in sugar they could walk by themselves. At the centre of it all stands the master confectioner, an artist, an expert of invention, a man who adjusts ingredients by instinct, gauging quantities by how the weather feels that day.

Master confectioners were artists, experts of invention, adjusting ingredients by instinct.

Woodcock at work

One such man was William Woodcock, whom wholesaler Thomas King claimed was the best sugar boiler in the trade. King had a grocer friend called Robert Robertson and they were thinking about setting up a sweet company. So King invited Robertson to see how Woodcock worked, partly to learn how to manufacture sweets, partly to assess the sugar boiler's suitability as a partner. Robertson had been surprised to hear how much material was wasted during the process, and wanted to see for himself. 'It was arranged that Woodcock should produce a boiling in my presence,' wrote Robertson later, 'and that all the sugar and glucose used should be accurately weighed, and the resultant boiling and scrap also checked and weighed. It did not quite turn out as planned.'

It was late 1906 when the two wholesalers arrived at Woodcock's small works in Queen's Road, East London to watch a boiling, the name for a single batch of work. Woodcock first took a couple of sugar loaves, heavy 30lb lumps bought from the Henry Tate refinery in nearby Silvertown, and pulverised them in a crushing machine. He put the powder into a vast copper pan, measured in some water and heated the mixture over the coke fire until the crystals melted. Glucose was the next ingredient. 'When it came to the glucose,' wrote Robertson, 'Woodcock merely plunged his hands into the barrel, brought out a lump and said this is 28lbs. With that I had to be content.' An industry so dependent on chemistry was hardly, then, a scientific business.

Together the sugar, glucose, water and copper pan weighed a hundredweight. Woodcock divided the mixture into two pans and, using the coke fire, brought

Plain Drops

A recipe from William Woodcock's recipe book.

25-lbs Sugar
12-lbs Glucose
1 Gallon Water

Method
Do not put in too much water as you lose time waiting for it to boil.

Cheap goods
Allow 6 oz acid, 1½ oz essence or 1 oz oil

Better goods
Allow 8 oz acid and a little more essence.

both to the boil. He then combined the two boils in one pan and heated it further. By now the boiling was firm enough to be tipped out onto a large metal slab, which had been dusted with starch to minimise sticking. The chill of the slab cooled the material enough for it to be worked by hand. Woodcock added colour and flavour – in this case to create *Raspberry Drops* – and then fed the mixture through 1¼ inch rollers, turned like a household mangle, to create a strip from which the sweets could be cut.

The work was hot, hard and heavy. Though some of the processes appeared random, the sweets were delicious. Robertson saw that King had made a good decision in recommending Woodcock as confectioner for their business – and the availability of Woodcock's machinery would save them a lot of money. Their new sweet company was taking shape.

How to make sweets

'Sugar turns liquid at 100°C, but it has to get hotter before work starts. A finger, licked and crack-nailed, was the dipstick of choice for many old hands. (It's not as painful as it sounds, not if you first wet your finger – the vapourized water forms a protective vacuum.) Old hands gauged temperatures by sight, using a variety of tests. Between 107°C and 110°C the syrup gets tacky, forming threads when pressed between finger and thumb. At around 112° comes the 'blow' state: dip the round end of a skewer in the syrup and you can blow a sad bubble. At 'feather' stage (115°) the bubble bursts, leaving flossy threads floating in the air (which gives us the simple principle behind candyfloss). And soon we're in business. At 118° is soft ball; 121° hard ball, when a pea-sized blob moulded between finger and thumb and thrown on the floor should bounce – perfect for caramels and butterscotch – and, no doubt, some great fun when the boss wasn't watching. At around 137° comes soft crack, when syrup dropped into cold water hardens immediately, cracking and sticking to the teeth when chewed. Another 17° (between 154° and 160°) and it becomes hard crack, as brittle and translucent as glass, perfect for boiled sweets. Well, you and I call them sweets, the trade prefers 'deposited boilings' – technically correct but hardly suitable for the soft sell. Control is vital. At 161° the syrup yellows, turning into barley sugar. A spot of bleach would be sufficient to fix that, though a drop of colouring could easily suffice to hide any defects. But any more boiling and the stuff becomes black jack – useless for anything.

'Turned out on to a slab (greased by lard, olive oil or petroleum jelly), colours and flavourings were added and the molten gunge was kneaded, turned, folded and thumped a hundred times while it cooled. After being rolled out into an elongated sausage – or 'rope' as they called it – pieces were snipped off with oiled scissors, the flattened ends giving a sharp-cornered pillow shape to the sweets.

'By pressing two or three or more lumps of molten sugar together prior to rolling out, all kinds of patterns could be obtained. Stripes and chequerboards were kids' stuff. And even a Union Jack didn't take much planning. With a good eye and a sense of humour, arty sugar-boilers could make all kinds of novelties – miniature slices of orange, for instance, formed with half a dozen roughly triangular lumps wrapped around by a sheet of 'peel' and then extruded and sliced.'

(From Nicholas Whittaker's Sweet Talk p18).

Arthur Sansome remembers

'I inherited, under great secrecy, the original recipe book for Sharps. It was a great big book with locks on it. One of the recipes in there dated back to the 1890s and explained how to rid your walnuts of maggots. What you did was put the walnuts in a pan, cover them with water then throw in a couple of handfuls of borax. You get them just warm and then sift them off, but you mustn't wash the borax off - it killed all the maggots. But surely people eating the toffee must have tasted the borax.' Arthur Sansome, chemist, who worked with Sharps then Trebor.

The four partners

A wholesale grocer with an idea to make sweets, a sugar boiler skilled but short of money, a retail grocer unhappy in his job — and a confectionery salesman, ambitious and alert.

Thomas King *wholesale grocer*

Thomas Henry King was born in 1869 near Limehouse in the old East End of London. His father worked as an unskilled labourer, a vulnerable job in a worsening economy, so the family often moved lodgings. By the start of the twentieth century, now in his thirties, King had moved up in the world, taking his wife and three daughters to the more comfortable suburb of Leytonstone. There at 11 Percy Road they lived a steady, church-going middle class life. Though he described himself as a wholesale grocer, King also worked as a travelling salesman for margarine – the new wonder product from Holland – and continued to set up businesses throughout his life. It's fair to assume it was King's entrepreneurial nature, rather than his Edwardian respectability, that attracted Woodcock. This ability to spot opportunities and gather teams set the new business on course.

William Woodcock *sugar boiler*

William Baglin Woodcock came from the old East End. He was born in 1852 within one of the rougher parts of Limehouse. His father was a house painter. By his late twenties Woodcock worked as a sugar boiler operating, like many such one-man businesses, from a workshop within the home. It was a precarious business: coke fires were unreliable and one mistake could ruin a whole batch, so wasting the money invested in sugar and glucose. Woodcock lived hand to mouth, a boisterous, hard-drinking fellow, whose first wife Elizabeth wrapped the sweets between delivering seven children. Elizabeth died in 1900. Now in his late forties with most of his children grown up, Woodcock married again and was able to move up in the world, to the new suburb of West Ham and then to Plaistow, where he set up work and home at 175 Queen's Road. But life remained hard. His second wife died and he married again, at 52, to a German widow from Islington. A new tax on imported sugar ate into his tiny margins. By 1905 he could no longer afford to buy raw materials. If he was to continue making sweets, he needed a backer to buy his sugar and then share in the profits. At this point he met King.

The first board meeting on 10th January 1907 was minuted by Robert Robertson. Its initial entry listed the four founders, along with their solicitor P R Gibbs.

Robert Robertson *retail grocer*

Robert Robertson's parents had already escaped the old East End by the time he was born in 1878. Like King and Woodcock, they migrated to the new East End, in their case West Ham. Robertson's father died when he was six, but left his wife enough money to open a grocer's shop in Rendel Road, Canning Town. Young Robertson got a far better education than Woodcock or King and by 1901, aged 22, he was helping his mother run the grocery. Two years later he married the daughter of a confectioner – interesting, given his subsequent career – and in 1906 they moved to 66 Boundary Road, Plaistow, buying the house 'on the Building Society never never method'. As an only son, Robertson was probably expected to take over the family grocer's, but his ambitions aimed far higher than a single shop.

Sydney Herbert Marks *sweet salesman*

Sydney Marks' father was the son of a rope merchant from Dorchester in Dorset; the family name Marks was an old west country surname. Sydney's father was selling 'oil and colour' and living with his family in Peckham, South London, when Sydney H Marks was born in 1874. Within a few years the family was living in the old East End, in Stepney, and Sydney H Marks went on to become a salesman himself. He married Margaret Scruton and lived at 62 Antill Road, Bethnal Green. Their son Sydney John was born in 1900 and Alex in 1903. By now Sydney H Marks was a top salesman, soon to be 'Chief Traveller', for the established confectionery manufacturer Chappel in Bow. This young ambitious man decided, like each of the other founding families, to leave the old East End. He took his young family to 23 Lytton Road, Leytonstone, a leafy suburb not far from Epping Forest. From there he set out each day on his sales trips and before long, like the other future partners, he came to the attention of King.

Forming the company

Thomas King introduced Robertson, Woodcock and Marks to each other in 1906. Within months they had agreed terms and incorporated their business.

It all started with chess. Robertson was a keen member of the East London Chess Club; so was King. They would play at the twice weekly club meetings in Stratford, at each other's houses and in matches with other clubs. Perhaps King's mind drifted during one of these chess games in 1906. He'd recently been approached by Woodcock, who supplied sweets to his wholesale business and, out of the blue, had asked for a loan to buy sugar; business wasn't good and King could share in the profits. This idea didn't excite King. But over the chessboard he heard Robertson complain about being stuck in a small grocery shop when he'd rather be building something bigger, something that could contribute to his large mortgage.

This gave King an idea. Rather than bankroll Woodcock, why not set up their own confectionery business, combining Woodcock's manufacturing skills – and equipment – with Robertson's ambition and his own entrepreneurial verve?

Robertson and Woodcock agreed to discuss it, but neither seemed particularly keen; the neat young businessman and the rough old sugar boiler must have felt they had little in common. It was only when King introduced someone else into the equation – Sydney H Marks, the best salesman he knew – that the idea took off. Woodcock would provide the machinery and manufacturing expertise. Robertson would work full-time alongside him. Marks would manage sales, but retain his day job selling sweets for Chappel. King would serve as part-time chairman. And so it happened: the new business was named after its two full-time employees – Robertson & Woodcock – and incorporated on 4th January 1907 with a share capital of £430.

The board meets

The first board meeting took place six days later at King's house in Percy Road, where it was agreed to allot £150 of shares to Woodcock in payment for his machinery. Robertson was employed as Company Secretary on 30/- (£1.50) per week. Woodcock earned more, his salary increasing to five pounds per week by the end

Above: the Alexandra Temperance Hotel in Stratford High Street – home to the East London Chess Club where King met Robertson – was a teetotal club with billiard tables, dining rooms, lounges and bedrooms. Today the building houses a children's centre.

Company Limited by Shares.

Memorandum
AND
Articles of Association
OF
Robertson and
WOODCOCK LIMITED.

Right: only Woodcock's name appeared on the first draft of company documents sent to the printers, so Robertson's name had to be added by hand.

of 1907. Only these two, the named founders of the firm, worked full-time and received a salary. King kept himself free for his other entrepreneurial activities, retaining only an annual director's fee and, later on, sharing dividends with the other directors.

Marks agreed to 'serve the Company as Managing Director and Traveller to the best of his ability and devote as much time thereto as he possibly can.' His official employer, Chappel, did not realise their star salesman was moonlighting as director for a rival firm, even though he maintained this secret arrangement until 1913; Chappel even made an official complaint during this time that a Robertson & Woodcock salesman was taking business from them, without learning the culprit's name. Sydney H Marks was clearly a smooth operator.

Right: the Trebor Terrace plaque still stands on the front of the villas in Shaftesbury Road where the firm first set up business.

The name Trebor

Many people assume the founders reversed Robert Robertson's name to create the word Trebor, but this was just coincidence; the name already existed on their first premises.

To keep costs down, King first planned to run the new business out of Woodcock's workshop in Queens Road. But he hadn't factored in Mrs Woodcock, who forbade her home to be used. This setback proved a blessing as the company could never have grown so fast in so small a property. Instead, Woodcock found premises on Shaftesbury Road in nearby Forest Gate. A small building known as Trebor Works enclosed a stable-yard and was fronted by Trebor House, built in 1891, and a line of seven two-storey villas called Trebor Terrace. Company legend recounts that Sydney Herbert, when visiting the premises with Robertson, turned to his colleague and said, 'That word on the front of the house, Bob, is your Christian name and part of your surname spelt backwards.'

Backwards spelling was a common feature of East End slang. But this named link between premises and founder member was co-incidence. The name Trebor actually came from the site's builder, a Robert

Cooper, who went on to name his grandson R. Trebor Cooper. That said, the co-incidence may have helped seal the deal. Eleven years later the name was adopted as the company trademark.

The initial rent for Trebor Works was one pound a week, though – their eyes on costs – the partners sub-let space for five shillings a week to an engineer making machines for trimming wall-paper. This arrangement did not last long. 'He objected to paying rent so we had to clear

him out sharpish,' recalled Robertson; they found a better tenant in a local coal supplier who needed space to stable his horse.

The name Trebor remains on the site to this day. The factory has been converted into flats but upon their front wall still proudly stands the slogan TREBOR QUALITY SWEETS.

Below: this plan shows the original layout for the premises that Woodcock found in Forest Gate.

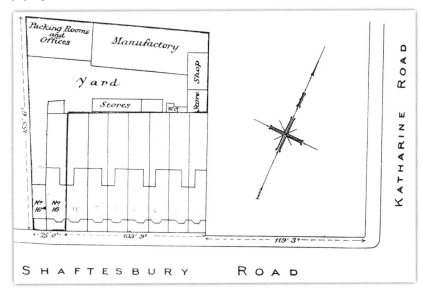

The new East End

All the founding directors came from families who had moved from the rough old East End to the emerging boroughs of West Ham and East Ham. Their migration – and success – mirrored the rise of this new East End.

BBC TV's long-running soap *Eastenders* is famous for being gritty and glum – apt attributes for the mythical East London in which it is set. The 'East End' has always been so. Given the prevailing westerly winds of Britain, the eastern sides of its cities traditionally housed the poor, where they could enjoy the fumes blown across from the fires of the well-heeled 'Westenders'. But in nineteenth century London the eastern side was doubly freighted with poor for it housed the docks to which the goods from the world's greatest empire came home. By 1868 five mighty docks had been built on the marshy ground east of the City of London, from St Catherine's by the Tower of London to the Royal Victoria Docks down river in Woolwich. These docks were vast consumers of manpower, with thousands of workers needed to empty and fill the ships, and with these dockers came a myriad of supporting activity – from importers and warehouses, chandlers and shipbuilders to markets, ale houses and whores.

This working population was squeezed into the dark slums that spread from the city walls in the west to the River Lee in the East. This was the 'old' East End – the lair of Fagin, Oliver Twist and Jack the Ripper – much of it a nightmarish bedlam of open sewers, cheap gin and eight to a room. The streets of Stepney, Shadwell, Wapping and Limehouse were no place for the shy or the rich, but they were handy for walking to work at the docks and, in a city expanding at breakneck speed, offered easy accommodation for the poor or the newly arrived.

Yet the docks were not to last. Maybe the magnificence of their engineering symbolised the pride of those about to fall, for the cost of unloading in the City led many ships to use the cheaper docks downstream at Tilbury. By 1888 two of the larger docks, the West India and the East India, had gone out of business. With local work receding, there was less need to suffer the indignity of living in the old East End.

Opened up by the railway

Meanwhile Eastern London, further out from the old East End, was exploding with new industry. During the later nineteenth century, this spurred the creation of a 'new' East End, built upon the marshland around

Left: the crowded streets of the old East End featured characters like the cat's meat man, seen here in 1901, who sold rotten meat for feeding animals.

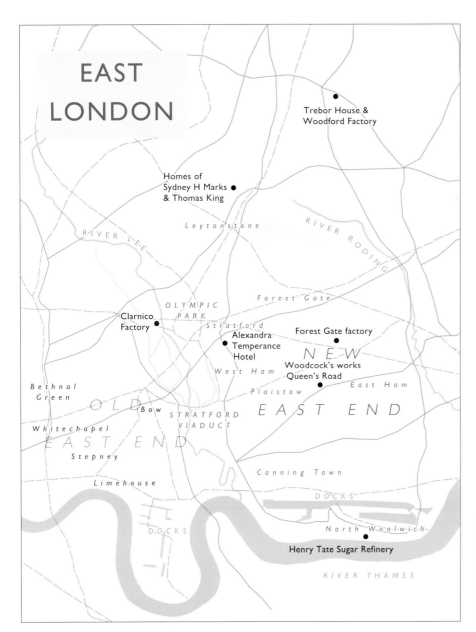

EAST LONDON

Trebor House &
Woodford Factory

Homes of
Sydney H Marks ●
& Thomas King

R I V E R   L E E

L e y t o n s t o n e

R I V E R   R O D I N G

F o r e s t   G a t e

*O L Y M P I C
P A R K*

Clarnico ●
Factory

S t r a t f o r d

Alexandra
● Temperance
Hotel

Forest Gate factory

N E W

Woodcock's works
Queen's Road

W e s t   H a m

E a s t   H a m

*B e t h n a l
G r e e n*

P l a i s t o w

E A S T   E N D

O L D

B o w   *S T R A T F O R D
V I A D U C T*

W h i t e c h a p e l

E A S T   E N D

S t e p n e y

C a n n i n g   T o w n

L i m e h o u s e

D O C K S

D O C K S

N o r t h   W o o l w i c h

Henry Tate Sugar Refinery

R I V E R   T H A M E S

Left: *between the River Lee and the River Roding arose the new East End. Smart new boroughs such as East Ham and Plaistow grew around the railway lines which had punched eastwards from central London during the mid-nineteenth century.*

West Ham and East Ham. In 1839 the Eastern Counties Railway reached Stratford. In 1847 a new branch went south towards the river at North Woolwich, so opening up Canning Town, Custom House and Silvertown. Further lines criss-crossed East London. With the trains came business, and people. West Ham's population rose fifteen times during the latter half of the nineteenth century; East Ham's increased from 2,858 to 96,018 over the same period.

Right: *Rothsay Road, just three streets north of the firm's first factory at Forest Gate, was typical of the more comfortable housing emerging in the new East End.*

Right: the Stratford viaduct built by the Eastern Counties Railway enabled trains to cross the marshland around the River Lee and open up the new boroughs of West Ham and East Ham.

Such headlong growth matched gold rush towns, but the emerging borough leaders were determined that housing should be much better than in the old East End. There was certainly demand for better accommodation; the railway ensured that middle-class commuters could now speed through the grime to their jobs in the City. As a result there arose suburbs like Leytonstone, Forest Gate, Plaistow and Manor Park – line after line of clean, comfortable terraced housing. But not just for the well-to-do. Their occupants were also railway engineers and policemen, skilled artisans and gaffers in the gas works, people who served the businesses opening up across the new East End.

Families on the move

We like to think we live today in a time of change and opportunity. But for sheer transformation of living conditions, we hardly match the change experienced by our late Victorian forebears. Town-sized communities appeared out of nowhere. Within a few years people moved from living beside open sewers to having their own bathrooms. But you had to make your own good fortune and, if need be, travel in search of it. Of the founding partners in this story, the Marks family travelled from Dorset to South London, to Stepney and Bethnal Green in the old East End then out to leafy Leytonstone. The Woodcocks went from Limehouse in the old East End up to County Durham in northern England, then to Camberwell in South London and back to Limehouse before moving up to the new comfort of Plaistow. Thomas King also made the move from Limehouse to Leytonstone, while Robert Robertson's parents had already left the old East End by the time that he was born.

There's nothing like tough origins to fuel ambition. The hunger to better themselves must have generated the remarkable energy that these founding partners brought to the new venture. Once they'd settled in the new suburbs around Stratford, they were determined to maintain this level of comfort for future generations; hence the drive to create a business of lasting value to their family, and a business which provided its workers – for the first time – with sufficient security to make the horrors of the old East End a distant memory.

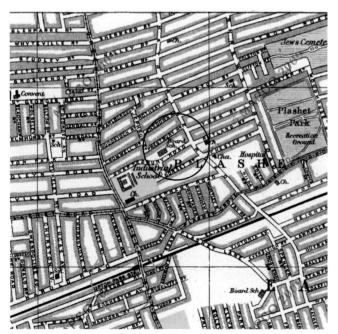

Below: the firm's first premises in Forest Gate sat where Shaftesbury Road met Katherine Road, beside the Board School marked in the black circle. Woodcock's home factory in Queen's Road (blue circle) was a few minutes walk away, as seen in this 1908 A–Z London streetmap.

Production starts

Though its sweets were popular from the start, Robertson & Woodcock suffered the financial and human stresses of any new business. It overcame these and prospered. Then World War One erupted.

Everyone has donned their best clothes for this works photo from 1908. Robert Robertson (left) and William Woodcock (right) flank six of the women who worked for the firm.

Woodcock had struggled to run his own sweet business, partly because he was a poor businessman, but also because 1901 saw the arrival of an import tax of four shillings and twopence on each hundredweight of sugar. By 1908 this tax was down to one shilling and tenpence, such a big drop – given sugar was the firm's main expense – as to boost the profitability of the new company.

Even so, starting a confectionery business in those days did not demand extensive capital. Anyone with sufficient money to buy a slab, a set of rollers and a coke fire could set up as a sugar boiler. In this case Woodcock provided much of the plant and machinery for free, in return for shares in the company. So the four partners, none of them rich, were able to launch their venture without risking their livelihoods.

Sweet making in Britain was on the brink of a technological leap. In 1906, methods of production were little different from a century before, hence the cheap ticket of entry, but soon they were to advance on a wave of mechanisation and quality control. The new Robertson & Woodcock was well placed to ride this wave. From its first boilings onwards, the new firm set out to supply working-class families with good sweets at low prices. (There were plenty of bad sweets available.) Such families might earn between one pound and thirty shillings a week. A child might get sixpence pocket money a week, enough to buy a lot of sweets. With often four ounces of sweets to the penny, even a farthing (quarter of a penny) could bring a fistful of treats.

Production commences

The early days were not glamorous. Woodcock set about building a coke stove in the new premises, creating a circular furnace from bricks which he laid over fixed fire bars, lined with bevelled fire-bricks and topped with cast iron plates to hold the copper boiling pans. On 12th December 1906 he ran out of fire-bricks.

Robertson was then moving his young family into their new house in Plaistow, so Sydney H Marks came in to help. 'Mr Marks set off on his bike,' recalled Robertson, 'for we all rode bikes in those days, but three dozen fire-bricks were too much and his rear tyre blew out. So he had to call in the services of a passing coster and his shay.' (A street trader with his horse and cart).

Once settled into his house, Robertson came back to help Woodcock as labourer – mixing mortar, carrying bricks – and as carpenter for the large flat slabs on which the sweets were rolled and finished. As soon as they had built the equipment, they bought their first hundredweight of coke from the coalman renting their stables, engaged two girls to finish the sweets Woodcock boiled, and started business.

Woodcock soon proved his worth as a sugar boiler. Most popular early on were his *Rock Allsorts*. These required thirteen separate boilings: eleven of different types of rock and two of plain toffee, mixed together into seven pound tins. It took all day to create one batch. Drops of various flavours, particularly raspberry, were standard at first, as were sugar sticks, eight inches long and a quarter of an inch thick, which sold for one farthing each. Other lines included *Cokernut Candy*, *Cokernut Ice*, *Tip-Top Cream*, *Indian Cream*, *Cokernut Chips* and *Stick-Jaw*. There was even a sweet called *Tobacco*, made of thread coconut coloured with cocoa shell powder, the use of which has long been banned, even from cattle feed.

The first summer of the new business, 1907, was a hot one. It can't have been fun with all the heat coming off the stoves and the air full of dust, starch and sugar powder. But orders were now coming in and, despite the heat, Woodcock and the others worked hard to make all the popular lines. 'The only line Woodcock would not make on really sticky days,' said Robertson, 'were the *Farthing Sugar Sticks*.' But these were the new company's most popular product. London children were very keen on such *Farthing Dips*. Each quarter penny bought a thin stick wrapped in coloured paper. If they found a red line running through it, they could claim the prize of a much larger stick weighing about quarter of a pound. Shopkeepers received the winning sticks separately, so they could arrange 'distribution' of the prizes as they wished.

C A Fletcher remembers

'Our first line was *Mixed Drops* and I can remember how as a representative I was handed a small two-ounce sample bottle to introduce our goods to the trade, being told that the price was 1/3d (7p) for a 7lb tin, with a penny deposit on the latter. Our next line was a farthing *Sugar Stick* and, following this, a real winner called *Rock Allsorts* which contained all kinds of striped rock in small pieces and some broken toffee.' Mr Fletcher was first invited to join the company by Robertson in 1907. He continued with the firm until retiring in 1947.

Tough business practices

New manufacturing companies need revenue and scale, so the firm started distributing products from other sweet makers too. In May 1907 one such company, the Anglo-Swiss Milk Chocolate Company, offered to pay four guineas (four pounds and four shillings) to have their advertisement painted on the Robertson & Woodcock delivery van. But when Robertson had already commissioned the painting, Anglo-Swiss back-tracked, now saying they would only pay two guineas. The board was furious, not just at such sharp practice, but also at Robertson's failure to get the agreement in writing; it decided to scrap the sign-writing, bury the cost and stop distributing Anglo-Swiss products. So threatened, Anglo-Swiss quickly caved in and agreed to pay four guineas. The directors were learning valuable lessons about the rough and tumble industry they had entered.

Initial challenges

Board tensions and unexpected tax demands took their toll
in the first years of the firm.

The early years were tough for Robertson & Woodcock. During 1907 the two
named founder members worked all hours to get the business going, helped by
two new sugar boilers – a man called George Webb and Woodcock's son Alfred.
But orders fluctuated and in June 1907 the incomers had to be put on shift work.
Board minutes show frequent arguments between Woodcock and his fellow
directors; they weren't keen on him making cash from selling sweets to factory
visitors; he frequently complained about his wages, fees, bonuses and working
conditions. Several times he threatened to sell his shares, then changed his mind.
His obstreperousness could partly be blamed on the stress of creating most of
the firm's products, but his drinking and argumentative nature cannot have helped.

Though Robertson was a neat man, with a good education and background
in wholesale, he does not appear to have maintained good records at that time.
Little account was kept of raw materials brought into the factory or of output
from the boiling room. And he was not alone. King would take finished product

Delivery by horse and cart

At first the company limited itself
to the London area. This offered
plenty of shops and stomachs, and
could easily be reached by
salesman on bicycle or public
transport. More importantly, it
was within reach of the horse-
drawn delivery van. As Sydney J
Marks later wrote, 'Boilings in jars
and slip lid tins could not be sent
by rail, because of risk of damage.
As a result the horse figured very
largely in manufacturers' and
wholesalers' calculations.' The
firm had only one horse-van and
driver, who sometimes did not
return to Trebor Works until two
or three in the morning; after
stabling the horse, he would bed
himself down beside it, ready for
an early start a few hours later.

Horses, and distribution,
appear frequently in board
minutes from those years. June
1908 saw a new horse bought for
16 guineas; unfortunately it
proved unsuitable, so Sydney H
Marks suggested buying another;

the board would only agree to
renting one. In October 1908 the
van driver's weekly wages were
raised to 23/- (£1.15) and a van
boy was employed for 6/- (30p)
per week. In April 1909
Woodcock and the van driver
were reported to the board for

fighting while drunk. The driver
was docked one shilling in wages
for this 'breach of discipline',
while Woodcock was 'requested
to apologise – this he would not
do', though he did 'express regret'
later after King had left the
meeting to catch a train.

Driver B Fretwell seen with the firm's horses and van in 1910.

to sell through his other businesses without providing receipts. Woodcock was notoriously vague with figures and even Marks failed to insist on strict accounting.

"Those early board meetings were not exactly picnics." *Charles Cockerill*

Cockerill arrives

This led to an early shock when the Inland Revenue made a huge tax demand in 1908 – and the company had little way of knowing whether it had actually made a profit or loss for the time in question. Marks turned to an accountant called Charles Cockerill, whom he had met when Cockerill married Miss Chappel, the daughter of his employer. As Cockerill later wrote, 'A lack of accounting caused some inconvenience which rather came to a head when the Revenue authorities sent in a tax claim for profits which the company could neither admit or deny.' Cockerill created a balance sheet from scratch, sorted out their problems with the Inland Revenue, and in return got five shares and no payment. He then agreed to work as company accountant for an annual fee of one guinea (one pound and one shilling) and in 1913 became auditor and subsequently a company director; he remained a board member until the Second World War.

Cockerill later remembered those early board meetings as 'not exactly picnics' and described the four founding directors as 'not one of the happiest combinations'. Describing King as 'no fool, but foolish in some things', he recounted one occasion when King went to court for an injunction against a motion passed at a general meeting; he lost and 'was mulched in all the costs'. He described the role of the working directors as 'no sinecure', recalling the 'hard manual work of Mr Woodcock in the rough and tumble of the boiling room and the assidunity of Mr Robertson in his carpentry work, putting up new shelves when we were able to procure more space.'

Labour challenges

Gradually the workforce grew. Woodcock's team of sugar boilers expanded, now all working full-time. Salesmen were employed and more young women were taken on to finish the sweets. But greater turnover did not yet mean greater profits – and the directors proved tough in their handling of staff. In 1912, for example, the board reluctantly increased wages for Webb the sugar boiler, but sacked his fellow boiler Mr Newton so they could 'find a cheaper man'. One pay increase was accompanied by the removal of all holiday pay except Christmas Day and Good Friday. The van driver and his assistant once refused to work altogether unless they were paid 'union wages'.

'It was suggested that H Woodcock and J Millar sugar boilers in the employ of the Firm should have a week's holiday to be paid for same. This was agreed to. Mr Marks reported that Mr Nicholls a traveller in the Cos Employ had been found pilfering Goods from the Warehouse and selling same. After consideration the Board

Below: before the Trebor brandname appeared in 1921, the firm used its trading name Robertson & Woodcock.

agreed to retain Mr Nicholls but the goods taken had to be paid for.'
Minutes 28th July 1909.

On the other hand, the staff could be a handful. Salesman Mr Nicholls was caught 'pilfering sweets' from the company. A summons for debt had to be issued against Woodcock's son and fellow boiler maker Alfred. 1913 saw an unpleasant incident when 'George Moore, a carman in the Company employ, after returning from a journey to Gravesend, failed to pay in his cash.' Later, in a 'drunken state, he refused to give up the cash to Mr Woodcock.' Although he paid up the cash the next day, 'he stated that he had lost all his gold (which he kept in a separate bag) amounting to nine pounds. He was therefore suspended and he promised to try and get a loan to enable him to pay the money.' He failed to do so. Later finding he had started working for a competitor, and still awaiting repayment, the directors instituted proceedings against him. But the bailiffs only succeeded in seizing property of Moore's wife, which had to be returned.

By 1913 Robertson & Woodcock was starting to look stronger. The board persuaded the landlord to build a new two storey building to provide extra capacity at Trebor Works. A new share issue raised the capital to £5,000. Marks started working full-time, focusing his considerable energy on the sales and transportation needs of the firm. The directors remained financially cautious – they turned down a quotation from the East Ham Corporation to provide mains electricity for £53, preferring instead to light the new workshops with the already out-of-date means of gas. On the other hand, they started paying themselves more significant dividends. The company was more robust, but could it survive four years of war?

Canny motorisation

A remarkable story is told by some otherwise unremarkable entries in the board minutes from 1915:

2nd March: Mr Marks proposes motor cars.
17th May: XYZ car hired at £530 pa for 12,000 miles, excess miles 9d per mile.
8th June: Purchase of Overland Car at cost not exceeding £400.
14th December: Mr Marks reports that all the horses have been sold, also vans.

Robertson & Woodcock was one of the first businesses to use motor transport in London. For several years its Overland Car 'The Pathfinder' – a light delivery van – was a novelty on the streets of the city.

Right: *one of the earliest delivery vehicles used by Robertson & Woodcock in London.*

War

World War One was a hard test for the fledgling firm. But thanks to some deft decisions, Robertson & Woodcock came through stronger than it might have expected.

Once war started, materials became tougher to source, with private importing banned and the tax on sugar raised fivefold in 1915 to nine and fourpence per hundredweight. By 1918 the industry received only a quarter of the sugar it got in 1915. The Government set maximum prices for sweets and banned salesmen from travelling; the firm put them to work in the factory instead. In some quarters it was even seen as unpatriotic to eat sweets: among the London County Council's wartime commandments, just between DON'T GO TO PICTURE PALACES and DON'T RIDE IN TRAMS UNNECESSARILY was the stark warning DON'T EAT SWEETS.

Fear of air raids led the company to take out air raid insurance and transfer important papers to a secure location. Though air raids between 1914 and 1918 posed far less threat than during the Second World War, they still caused 2,300 casualties in London and must have been terrifying.

Staff levels were hit by enlistment; in 1916 the board reported that the business was being run by the working directors 'despite the absence of staff', who now numbered only twelve. The directors decided to pay an allowance to all serving employees. When salesman C. A. Fletcher was called up in 1916, the firm paid his mother a pound a week while he served; he was also granted a payment of £58 in 1918 for serving. While Woodcock and King were too old to fight, Robertson became liable in 1916 but was never called up. Marks received call up papers in June 1918, working at Ellis' Wire Rope Works before returning to the firm in November the same year.

News came in June 1918 that F Hare, a company driver, had been killed in action. The board decided to make a payment of £20 to his parents. Woodcock's son Alfred received a war pension for a shrapnel injury. But overall it appears Robertson & Woodcock was relatively untouched by the wider tragedy; the much larger firm Rowntree alone lost two hundred employees, not counting the limbless and shell shocked who might never work again.

Below: compulsory rationing did not start in Britain until near the end of World War One. Sugar was the first commodity to be restricted, in December 1917. Later there were also coupons for meat, butter and margarine, jam, bacon, lard and tea.

Smart management

The firm made some good decisions during the war. At Marks' encouragement, the horses were replaced by a motorised delivery van – one of the first to be seen on London streets. In response to dwindling supplies of sugar, Robertson even set up a chocolate sweet department. It's hard to tell from the board minutes how precisely the firm's finances were affected by the war. In May 1917 Marks reported that profits were down considerably, but by July that year the company was confident enough to propose a 15% dividend and buy a life governorship of the local St Mary's Hospital; philanthropy is usually one of the first things dropped in straightened times, but not here. By January 1918 the half year dividend had risen to 25%.

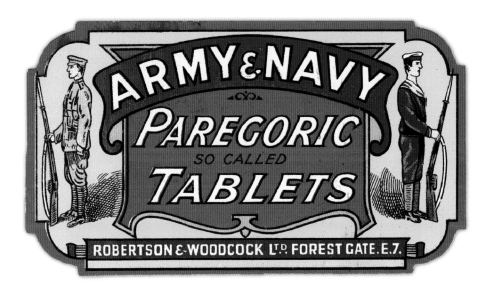

Unlike many sweet firms – Fry's, for example, was taken over by Cadbury – Robertson & Woodcock survived the war well.

> The secretary reported receipt assessment for Excess Profits amounting to £392-17-0 for the six months ending 31 Dec 1914. This sum was considerably in excess of what had been anticipated. Minutes, 2nd May 1916

Company accountant Clive Cockerill later said that the firm was affected badly by wartime taxation: World War One 'helped the company in the way of profits, but the introduction of the Extra Profits Tax hit it very hard indeed, as the standard profit year was so low owing to the lean years while the company was getting onto its feet. Thus the major part of the increased profits went to the government.' Not maybe an ideal outcome for the hardworking directors, but definitely a contribution to the war effort.

Above left: *'paregoric' referred to a camphorated tincture of opium, famed for centuries for its soothing qualities. This unsurprisingly proved attractive to soldiers during WWI, just like benzedrine during WWII and cannabis during the Vietnam War. These popular post-war Army & Navy tablets were 'so-called' paregoric because the opium content had, by then, been removed.*

Charitable work from the start

When profits allowed, the directors were keen to practise philanthropy. During World War One the firm supported its local St Mary's Hospital. Through the 1920s, even though modernisation and fluctuating sales hampered profits, company maintained its donations. Those benefitting included Dr Barnardos, Lady Pearson's Fund, Dr White's homes, the Forest Gate YMCA, the East Ham and Queen Mary's hospitals and, of course, the Confectioners Benevolent Fund.

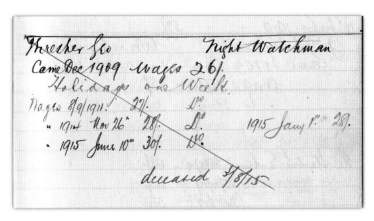

Left: *a sad glimpse into the war comes in this page from a staff log from Clarnico – a fellow East London sweet company later bought by the firm. George Thresher joined as a night watchman in December 1909. His wages rose steadily to thirty shillings a week by June 10th 1915. He was then called up to fight. By 3rd August he was dead, presumably in France. In total some 396 Clarnico workers went to war; 69 were severely wounded and 39 were killed – a casualty rate of nearly one in three.*

1919–1945

GOING NATIONAL

These were crucial decades. New machinery enabled the firm to sell good sweets at lower prices. A fresh generation, in the form of Marks' son Sydney, set its sights beyond London and the southeast. As a result, Trebor became a name nationwide.

Modern and mechanical

By the 1920s the firm had lost Woodcock, its creative kindling, but gained the main architect of its future success. Though barely out of his teens, Sydney John Marks saw the need to seek out the best technology.

Nine days after the Armistice in 1918 signalled the end of war, the firm registered Trebor as a trade mark. Although the new brandname did not appear on products for another three years, when the Trebor Confectionery Company was registered in December 1921, Robertson & Woodcock was no longer the same company that had started back in 1907.

Woodcock was gone. William Woodcock, the master sugar boiler, around whose talent King had fashioned the business in the first place, whose rough ways spurred constant conflict with his politer partners, announced his retirement in April 1918. He was sixty six and exhausted after so many years of hard work. He sold his shares for £990 and received a pension of three pounds per week for ten years, along with a bonus of £100 and a further £200 'in consideration of past services'. Much of this money he spent on setting up his children in their own businesses, while he lived on until 1936.

As old blood left, new blood arrived. In late 1918 Marks' son Sydney John was due to leave the Officer Cadet Corps and study electrical engineering. His father persuaded him to spend a little time in the firm before college. He did so – and never left. He was still there fifty three years later when he retired in 1971.

New facilities, new machinery

'The business had advanced and increased despite a shortage of labour and raw materials. The outlook had been very black at the start of the year – no sugar to boil and only 12 employees. The Company then turned to products for which materials were available and the chocolate department was the result. It turned a large deficit into an increase of turnover of £18,000. Sugar supplies increased later in the year and led to an increase in business fuelled by an ever increasing demand for the goods we manufacture. Freehold of the works had been purchased. Employees totalled about 60 and efforts were being made to improve their terms and status. A dining room was planned and relations were cordial.' Minutes, December 1919.

Though sugar supplies remained tight, Robertson urged the firm to extend its factory and buy new machinery. First the directors bought the property at Forest Gate where they worked for £1500. In 1920 they installed electricity. Over the

HR Bailes remembers

'I started work at Robertson & Woodcock in March 1919, aged 14 years. It was a small factory in Forest Gate and they boiled sweets over coke fires: *Mixed Fruit Drops, Rock Allsorts, Pineapple Drops, Pear Drops.* Packed in 7lb tins, they sold at 4oz for 4d, and good lines they were too. We had one small motor van and we delivered our goods all over London. The once-a-year beano outing to Southend or Brighton was always a happy event and talked about for weeks after.' HR Bailes talked to Working Together magazine in the summer of 1969.

½D "Trebor" TREACLE TRUNCHEON ½D

A convoy of Robertson & Woodcock lorries gets ready to collect sugar from the London Docks so production can continue during the 1926 General Strike.

next few years they commissioned many plans for expanding the factory, though money for these was threatened by massive post-war tax demands. Even so, they were able to buy adjacent properties and gradually upgrade the facilities.

In 1923 a new block brought the factory's floor-space to 8,500 square feet, twice its pre-war capacity. The workforce at Forest Gate now numbered sixty. 1929 saw the completion of Block D and a further 9,000 square feet of accommodation. The top floor of this block was initially assigned to making chocolate goods – which Robertson had pioneered in 1918 – but demand for boiled sweets soon forced the firm to stop making chocolates.

Robertson and Marks worked well together. Along with the young Sydney J Marks, they had radical plans to modernise the company. In 1922 they replaced the old coke and gas boilers with modern steam boilers. Despite the expense, they installed state-of-the-art kit in the form of a Cochran Boiler and a No 5 Baker Perkins Continuous Cooker and Melting Pan. No longer need everything be done by hand. The firm was now at the forefront of sugar boiling technology.

> 'Mr Sydney Marks then reported on his experiences in two German factories … he recommended to concentrate on the ground floor the whole of the manufacture of hard boiled goods and satins and to use the upstairs floor of the factory for caramels and count goods … it would be best if gas stoves, which were expensive to run, were disposed with … he recommended the purchase of a Vacuum Cooking Machine and a Gabel Plastic Machine.'
> Minutes, 28th July 1924.

By 1925, at Sydney Marks' recommendation, the firm had bought new German machinery to mechanise processes and enable a wider range of high quality sweets to be produced – including satins, mixed fruit drops and bulls-eyes. Sweet prices had risen sharply since the war, but this efficiency meant the firm could actually sell them more cheaply.

Wholesalers feared such bold pricing might bankrupt the firm. Instead it ushered in an era of mass consumption. As Sydney Marks later wrote, 'It was the low cost of ingredients and the improvement in manufacturing and transport productivity in the 1920s and 1930s that gave consumers

Family business: sisters Gertie and Nellie Gooch are pictured here in 1919 with their friend Belinda Tyrie. Back then only around twelve women worked in the factory, employed on slab work and making lettered rock. They worked 50 hour weeks at 6½d per hour.

Sydney J Marks remembers

'When I joined Trebor we were without electricity, all the goods were made by hand and the craftsman ruled supreme. The boiling room consisted of six pairs of coke fires, each pair run by a team of three women. In the winter they let the fires burn for a time to warm up the place before putting on the copper pans, the room filled with sulphurous fumes and we all had a jolly good cough before starting the day's work. We had no electricity, steam or cold water plates; everything was done by hand. They produced between ten and fifteen tons a week depending on whether they were making, say, *Pear Drops* through hand-turned drop machines, or patterned rocks depicting pineapples and strawberries. We were the first in many things.

'Sometimes a van, after unloading sugar, could not get under the archway formed by two rooms that spanned the Shaftesbury Road entrance. So on the cry "All Out", everyone downed tools, rushed into the yard and jumped into the van. Down went the springs, out went the van! Old Harry got his van out of our yard and the ton and a half of Trebor beauties walked jokingly back to work.' Sydney Marks recalling his early days at Forest Gate during his 60th Anniversary party in 1978.

low-priced confectionery. That is when high sweet consumption really became established in this country.' But as raw material prices dropped, so competition rose. The market became flooded with very cheap sweets. The firm responded with a new grade of boilings under the name Boleyn Pure Sweets, selling initially at two-pence for a quarter pound. These did well.

As the 1920s came to a close, the company remained a small player within the British sweet industry, but it had grown massively since formation just thirteen years before. More importantly, Trebor was an agile, forward-thinking business, eager to hitch its fortunes to new machines and new markets.

Right: *a 1920s portrait of the toffee boiling section at the Sharps factory in Maidstone, a business later acquired by the firm. Once each boil of toffee was cooked, it was poured out onto the long benches for cutting.*

Right: *The firm introduced the Boleyn grade of boilings to compete with the cheap sweets encouraged by lower sugar prices in the 1920s. The name came from a local landmark, the Boleyn Castle, reputedly associated with Henry VIII's wife Anne Boleyn, which later gave its name to West Ham's football ground (also known as Upton Park). The Boleyn range included satins, mixed fruit drops and bullseyes, presented in large glass jars. Despite the high quality, the firm was able to sell Boleyn goods for £40 per ton, compared to £80 per ton for Trebor sweets.*

BOLEYN
PURE SWEETS
4 OZS 3 D.
ROBERTSON & WOODCOCK LTD LONDON, E.7.

Mr Sydney goes to Germany

Having rejected engineering college to join his dad's firm, Sydney J Marks put his technical interests to practical use.

Bill Coller remembers

'I can remember climbing onto the playground shed in the big boys' playground and looking over the wall. The smell of boiled sweets was with us all day. Sometimes during playtime a resonant female voice would yell out something like: "Look out" – and over the wall came sweets that had stuck together during the making, wrapped in newspaper. They would hit the playground with a smack and scatter all over – but we never minded a bit of dirt on our free sweets in those days!' Bill Coller went to Shaftesbury Road Primary School next door to the Forest Gate factory from 1924 until 1928.

In 1924 he travelled to Germany to spend several months studying how German sweet firms used modern machinery. But he nearly didn't get there. As the company magazine later reported, 'There happened to be a pilot strike, which meant the director of the aviation company was piloting. On the second lap, from Brussels to Cologne, he joined the pilot with the intention of navigating. Greatly to his and the pilot's horror, the only map in the cockpit turned out to be a Michelin road map. This is possibly the only time a pilot has been directed to "turn right at the next crossroads."'

Once safely arrived, he stayed with a family called Hiller and worked in their confectionery factory. Not surprisingly so soon after the war, there was some ill-feeling towards the English. As John Marks explains, 'When

Left: a model of the first continuous high boiled sugar sweet forming machine, made by Albert Henkel, which reached Forest Gate in 1924. This Hansella Plastic Machine formed sweets from a rope of 'plastic' or malleable sugar fed into it. Such high tech machinery replaced the hand-turned machines used previously.

grandfather was working on the hot sugar line, they would steal his gloves. But he wouldn't stop, even though his hands got badly burned and he got sugar poisoning.' This didn't prevent the Marks and Hiller families starting a friendship that spanned generations. John stayed with them during his National Service in 1949 and said, 'It was at the Hillers that my brother and I learnt to make Trebor mints.'

At the Henkel factory in Viersen, Sydney discovered the new Hansella forming machinery, while at Krefeld he saw the latest vacuum-cooking equipment. On returning to Forest Gate, he persuaded the board to re-organise the factory around these new machines. With vacuum-cooking, the firm could now make boiled sweets much faster and more cheaply, while the Hansella machines allowed production of sweets such as satins, which had seldom previously appeared in London and the Southeast. These enhancements, helped by lower sugar prices, enabled the company to produce high quality boilings at low cost – perfect for expanding market share during the 1920s.

Below right: this advert appeared in the Confectionery Journal, 14th July 1927. Trebor introduced glass jars during the mid 1920s to replace the old seven pound tin. By 1930 the company minutes reported the firm washed up to 4,000 jars every day.

Left: Elizabeth Cornford joined the firm in 1920 as a clerk. At first all business was transacted in cash, but soon she got to type out the first wholesale invoice.

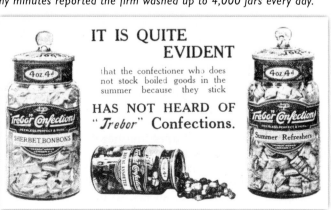

IT IS QUITE EVIDENT that the confectioner who does not stock boiled goods in the summer because they stick HAS NOT HEARD OF "Trebor" Confections.

The Thirties

This decade saw the arrival of iconic products such as *Refreshers* and *Extra Strong Mints*, a workforce now in its hundreds and the first foreign sales. The small sugar boiling firm from Forest Gate was becoming a big player in sweets.

'Mr SJ Marks moved that in the opinion of the Board the time has arrived to make provision for employees who reach an age when they are no longer able to work, provided that a suitable scheme can be formulated to carry this into effect; employees to be allowed to subscribe up to 5% of their annual salary and the firm to subscribe an equal amount. The estimated cost to the firm was £500, though this depended on the number of employees.' Minutes, 18th December 1929.

At their board meeting on 18th December 1929 the Robertson & Woodcock directors considered a plan for the company's first worker's pension scheme. This showed their confidence in the business and its long-term prospects. Profits were growing steadily, as were the factory premises and the workforce. The fruits of mechanisation were clear to see. As the 1930s unfolded, the forces that had propelled growth in the previous decade – particularly the ambition and ability of Sydney H Marks and his son – were to maintain this relentless pace.

Mints arrive

'S J Marks reported that a scheme to advertise and help the sales of 1d Extra Strong Mints had been adopted. The scheme had been devised by Messrs Gale & Polden and the cost was about £500.' Minutes, 28th July 1937.

In 1929, thanks to its connection with the German company Hiller, Robertson & Woodcock became the first British manufacturer to produce compressed sugar tablets directly from dry raw materials. The pharmaceutical industry had already compressed powder to make pills and tablets, but the process was new to British confectionery. German engineering enabled peppermints to be made and wrapped automatically – which was to boost Trebor's fortunes in the 1930s. In 1935 the firm launched what was to become its most iconic product – the Trebor *Extra Strong Mint* – which initially took its place, like *Fruit Refreshers*, among the traditional weight lines; the first mints were priced at forty shillings per hundredweight, packed in four pound jars. By 1937, as the Minutes show, the firm was prepared to spend £500 on advertising them.

Launched in 1935, the Extra Strong Mint was to become one of Trebor's most famous brands, still strong today.

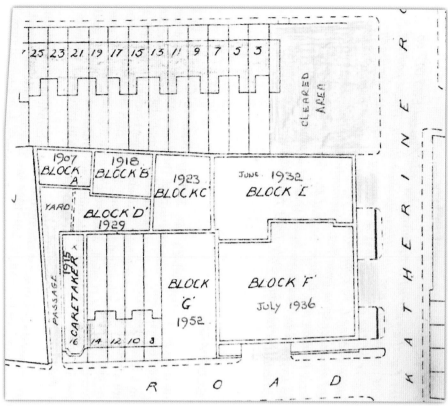

Above: from its original Block A in 1907, the factory at Forest Gate expanded up to 1936 through a series of ever larger developments, with a further Block G added in 1952.

Expansion and innovation

The streets around Forest Gate enjoyed few moments of peace from the noise of builders during the 1930s. Board minutes talk constantly of new building projects: 1932 saw the completion of Block E with 12,000 square feet of extra factory and office space; in 1933 appeared a glass roof on top of Block D to provide more offices. Then in 1935 Robertson and Sydney J Marks took another trip to Germany. On their return, suitably enthused, they drew up plans to rebuild the Forest Gate factory at twice its previous size. This meant knocking down four houses in Katherine Road and building a new 580,000 square foot space. Messrs Rice & Sons won the building contract for £30,009. But as soon as the new space opened in 1938, it found itself operating at full capacity so another factory was needed. This time the directors looked outside London. In May 1939 the board considered building a facility at Chesterfield in Derbyshire. The arrival of war delayed this project, which is described in a later chapter.

Technical innovations continued. From 1930 the company started receiving glucose in bulk, delivered to Forest Gate by a big, shiny glucose tanker. In 1936 the board employed the Institute of Industrial Psychology to investigate better ways of weighing up and labelling jar

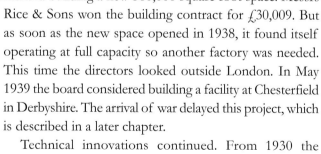

Left: the firm pioneered the handling of glucose from tankers, receiving in 1930 London's first ever delivery of glucose in bulk. The older building behind the lorry is most probably the original Trebor works.

Above: the Forest Gate factory in the 1930s.

goods; this was an early instance of Trebor's later prolific use of consultants to pursue efficiency through new ways of working. The large new factory wing of 1938 also enabled the company to adopt fresh machinery and layout, inspired partly by what Sydney J Marks saw in Germany and partly by the advice of consultants.

As the Trebor brand grew, so Robertson & Woodcock relied less on selling products from other firms. Such factoring had always been a major part of the business – inspired perhaps by the wholesaling background of Thomas King – and it still contributed strongly to turnover as late as 1938. The complexity of these activities had led to the firm contracting out delivery from 1928. But as the Trebor lines proliferated, with their greater profit margin, so the firm focused more on its own products. This made distribution easier. At the same time, Trebor products were gaining popularity beyond Southeast England. All these trends demanded a more considered delivery system. By the late 1930s, the firm was busy building up its own fleet of lorries.

Denmark first: Thorvald Pedersen of Copenhagen became Trebor's first overseas customer in 1930. He later helped the firm overcome restrictions on importing sugar and glucose.

First export activities

'Mr SH Marks tabled the itinerary of his journey and reported that all arrangements had been made through Messrs Cook and Son Ltd and he would depart on the 22nd October and return in May next. Contact would be made with the company's Agents in Gibraltar, India, Burmah, Straits Settlements, Dutch East Indies, Australia, New Zealand and Canada. The Board decided that a grant in the sum of £500 be made towards expenses.'
Minutes, 31st August 1938.

If you asked an early employee of Robertson & Woodcock about exports, they would probably assume you meant selling sweets in Manchester or Glasgow. Most sweet firms back then served only their locality. But with the arrival of the Trebor brand, the company started spreading beyond the south of England. Moreover, Sydney J Marks took an international perspective from the start. During the 1920s he visited sweetmakers on the Continent and, while he knew Germans manufacturers were more technically advanced, he could see the possibilities for export trade. Even so, the firm avoided selling to Germany, fearing to annoy the German manufacturers whose technical expertise it needed for acquiring and maintaining machinery.

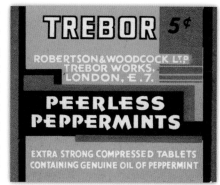

With currency amended, the firm's UK packaging worked overseas.

Exports grew gradually to reach 400 tons per annum by 1939.

The first actual foreign sales came through a man who was to play a long-standing role in the fortunes of Trebor – a Dane called Thorvald Pedersen of Copenhagen. He started selling Trebor count lines to Danish customers in 1930 (and later helped the firm bypass restrictions on importing raw materials). But mostly the firm worked through specialist exporting merchants in London, Liverpool and Manchester. Exports grew gradually through the decade to reach 400 tons per annum by 1939. Not a tremendous quantity, but the directors were at least starting to look further afield, particularly within the British Empire. In 1937 Sydney H Marks visited South Africa and reported back to the board on prospects for trade there. Then in late 1938 he planned more ambitious research in the form of a round the world trip. The imminence of war understandably put this trip – and all such ideas – on hold.

Board changes

'Mr King's position was then discussed by the Directors. Mr Merrett stated that Mr King having made a composition with his creditors he could no longer merit the confidence of the board and that a director so doing should not be allowed to stand or continue in that capacity…It was agreed that seven days be granted for Mr King's answer. Mr Merrett pointed out that failing resignation, it would be necessary to take other means of terminating Mr King's Directorship.' Minutes, 25th July 1933.

Left: *a van from the 1930s.*

HC Merrett joined as an accountant during the 1930s and rose to become chairman.

Big changes were sweeping the board. On 28th July 1933 Thomas King resigned as chairman and director. This was prompted by failures in his businesses outside the firm which led to him being declared bankrupt. The other directors felt he could no longer remain part of Robertson & Woodcock so they encouraged him to resign. It was a sad development. Without King's initiative in gathering the founding directors, the firm would never have emerged. But outside the firm he never seemed able to muster the same commercial success – and those external failures eventually brought him down.

By October 1934 a new board had emerged. Sydney H Marks was now chairman and managing director. Robertson was secretary and accountant, Sydney J Marks was general manager, his brother Alex had joined the board as transport manager and Cyril Robertson (son of founder Robert Robertson) was works engineer. Control now lay entirely in the hands of the Marks and Robertson families.

Another important figure to emerge during this period was Mr HC Merrett, a chartered accountant who started guiding the firm's finances in 1931. He introduced systems suitable for what was now becoming a significant business and, as a reflection of the directors' confidence in him, started attending board meetings. In 1936 he became a director himself, the next year vice-chairman and subsequently served as the chairman. Merrett was one of several highly loyal and capable consiglieri to serve the family business over the years. Other important employees to emerge during this time were Allan Hurndell, head of buying, Sidney Bonner, chief engineer and Denis Hedley, service manager.

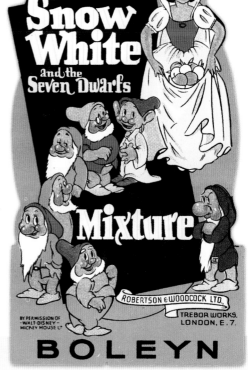

Clever marketing

These days most film producers rely on licensing deals to help fund their films. Back in 1938 it was not so common. So the firm was highly innovative when it bought the merchandising rights for Walt Disney's Snow White and the Seven Dwarfs. The characters appeared on the packaging, the film was a hit and children started exercising their muscles of pester power.

As the Minutes of 30th November 1938 reported: 'Mr SJ Marks reported purchase of Licence for a term of one year as from 1st December 1938, to use Snow White & The Seven Dwarfs for High Boilings, for the sum of £150. A licence fee of 20 /- per

Above and below: Snow White product to tie in with the Disney film.

ton of goods manufactured was payable but the sum of £150 prepaid was to be applied against the licence fees to be paid.'

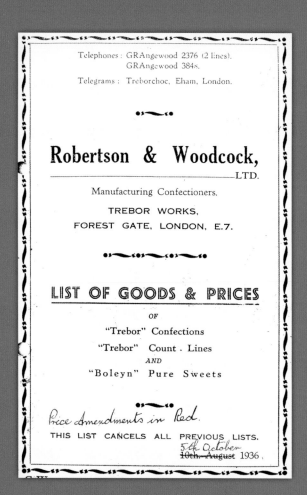

Robertson & Woodcock,
LTD.

Manufacturing Confectioners.

TREBOR WORKS,
FOREST GATE, LONDON, E.7.

LIST OF GOODS & PRICES
OF
"Trebor" Confections

"Trebor" Count . Lines
AND
"Boleyn" Pure Sweets

Price Amendments in Red.

THIS LIST CANCELS ALL PREVIOUS LISTS.

5th October
10th August 1936.

Vast product range

Open a Robertson & Woodcock wholesale price list from the mid 1930s and you find many hundreds of different products, at all types of price, size and quality. The Trebor Boilings, priced per pound in four to seven pound jars, include such treats as *Paradise Fruits*, *Imperial Butterdrops*, *Grannies Chest Tablets* and *Army & Navy Paregoric Tablets*. There are special lines such as *Butter Almonds* and fancy boxes of sixpence *Barley Sugar Soldiers* and decorated tins containing a pound of *Creamy Toffees*. The Trebor Count Lines of individually-priced sweets (rather than sweets weighed out from a jar) take up more catalogue than ever; with old-school names like *Foaming Fizz*, *Clickety Clicks* and *Raspberry Dab Suckers* alongside sweets more recognisable today such as *Lemon Refreshers* and *Black Jacks*. At the back you find what today would be called the 'value' ranges – the Boleyn Pure Sweets, sold for forty shillings or so per hundredweight. Here appear another three hundred lines, from *Pastilles*, *Rocks*, *Satins*, *Crunches* and *Fingers* to *Balls*, *Bullseyes*, *Rings* and *Toffees*.

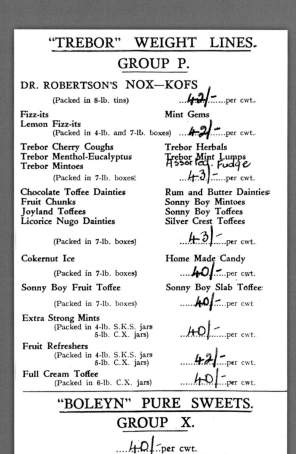

"TREBOR" WEIGHT LINES.
GROUP P.

DR. ROBERTSON'S NOX—KOFS

(Packed in 8-lb. tins) ... 42/- per cwt.

Fizz-its	Mint Gems
Lemon Fizz-its	

(Packed in 4-lb. and 7-lb. boxes) ... 42/- per cwt.

Trebor Cherry Coughs	Trebor Herbals
Trebor Menthol-Eucalyptus	Trebor Mint Lumps
Trebor Mintoes	Assorted Fudge

(Packed in 7-lb. boxes) ... 4.3/- per cwt.

Chocolate Toffee Dainties	Rum and Butter Dainties
Fruit Chunks	Sonny Boy Mintoes
Joyland Toffees	Sonny Boy Toffees
Licorice Nugo Dainties	Silver Crest Toffees

(Packed in 7-lb. boxes) ... 43/- per cwt.

Cokernut Ice   Home Made Candy

(Packed in 7-lb. boxes) ... 40/- per cwt.

Sonny Boy Fruit Toffee   Sonny Boy Slab Toffee

(Packed in 7-lb. boxes) ... 40/- per cwt

Extra Strong Mints
(Packed in 4-lb. S.K.S. jars
5-lb. C.X. jars) ... 40/- per cwt.

Fruit Refreshers
(Packed in 4-lb. S.K.S. jars
5-lb. C.X. jars) ... 42/- per cwt.

Full Cream Toffee
(Packed in 6-lb. C.X. jars) ... 40/- per cwt.

"BOLEYN" PURE SWEETS.
GROUP X.
... 40/- per cwt.

CRUNCHES	French Nut Cubes

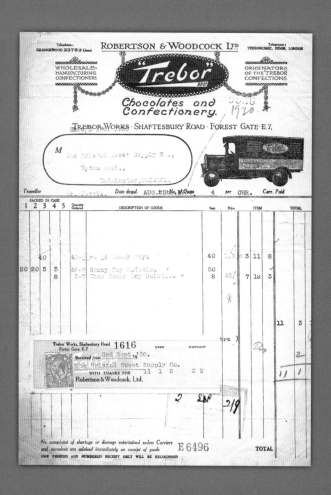

Sweet invention

Ever since William Woodcock surprised his fellow directors with miraculous inventions in sugar boiling, the firm depended on creative genius within the hot heart of the business.

One such expert was David Plaistowe, chief confectioner between 1949 and 1959. While visiting Germany in 1937 he got the idea for boiling a cream toffee far higher than normal, so making it crisp rather than soft. The only problem was that the firm's machines could not achieve this without burning the milk in the mixture. So he found a vacuum cooker which might work, persuaded a reluctant Sydney J Marks to invest £1,000 in buying one, and started trials. 'I made out the mixing I wanted and gave it to old Bob Paton,' Plaistowe later recalled. 'He said,

"David Plaistowe was the architect of all the firm's successful lines." *Clifford Broom*

"You can't do this – it's a caramel mixing." I said, "Yes it is, but try it for me." I gave him boiling heights as far as I could reckon them for a first batch. All went well and the batch was poured out on the slab. Bob's eyes started out of his head. He said, "You've got something here." The batch was at a firm crack height when tested in 60° F water and was beautifully smooth and creamy. We put a cushion die on the Hansella machine and ran the boiling through. Very little reached the jars in the weighing room as the girls ate most of it.'

Plaistowe made another batch of this light crisp toffee for the next sales meeting, but some salesmen proved reluctant to take samples of such a strange new product out on the road. Those that did, did well. Within weeks the new product was outselling the other lines. 'We worked as many hours as permitted, including every weekend, and still we could not meet the orders,' said Plaistowe. 'As usual all our competitors tried to copy our product, but they failed.' So was born the *Toffee Butters* which, together with *Extra Strong Mints*, became the company's most popular line in the late 1930s. Indeed the success of *Toffee Butters* in 1938 led to the firm gaining a considerable sugar ration during the war. Factory manager Clifford Broom later described Plaistowe as 'the architect of all the firm's successful lines. He made toffee that didn't stick to your teeth. He invented *Refreshers*. He was a magnificent confectioner.'

Creative genius: *David Plaistowe joined the firm in 1937 as works manager, rising to production manager then chief confectioner in 1949. The Trebor Magazine later described him as an 'artist in sugar.'*

BOLEYN THE ORIGINAL TOFFEE BUTTERS ARE BETTER THAN EVER

Try some yourself and taste the butter and milk in them

They are pure, wholesome sweets of outstanding merit and wonderful value at
2d. per qtr.

If you want your customers to come again, do not fail to ask them
"Have you tried Boleyn Toffee Butters ?"

This little effort on your part will bring you daily increased sales of this very popular line

Left: *the success of Toffee Butters in the late 1930s helped the firm secure a large sugar quota during the Second World War.*

1930s products

Perhaps it's the power of nostalgia, or the joy of seeing colour from a black and white age, but sweet wrappers from this period seem stylish and enticing.

"Brandname": until the 1940s the firm put its name Trebor into quotation marks.

Royal fever: the mid 1930s saw two bouts of kingly celebration with the Silver Jubilee of George V in 1935 and the Coronation of George VI in 1937. Like most sweet companies, Trebor hitched a ride with suitably branded products.

Targeting boys: *1930s wrappers were so skewed towards masculine pursuits, you might imagine girls didn't eat sweets. Even the 'delicately perfumed' varieties had boyish names like Jockey Club.*

Healthy properties: *medicinal claims were standard practice for attracting ailing adults.*

World War Two

The firm's incredible growth of the 1930s was now threatened by austerity and government control. But once again Trebor coped well with wartime. A new factory arose in Chesterfield, while Sydney J Marks' smart use of ration paved the way for fast expansion once war ended.

By 1939 the firm was flourishing as never before. Production ran at full capacity, even though factory space at Forest Gate had doubled just two years before. Sydney J Marks had spurred tremendous advances in mechanisation and working practices. His father was travelling the world, looking for overseas markets. There were more products than ever, more delivery lorries and more employees. But as the year progressed, and war became inevitable, the directors must have worried how hostilities would hinder this achievement. They remembered how a fledgling Robertson & Woodcock had survived the First World War, but the firm was now so much larger and had more to lose. Though few could then have foreseen how pervasive and prolonged this conflict would become, the board must have expected a hammering.

In practice, it didn't turn out too bad. Just as between 1914 and 1918, the firm proved adept at seizing opportunities out of the uncertainty of war, especially in distribution. During the First World War it set up one of London's first motorised delivery services. This time, the need to distribute products more nationally – and produce them more safely than in bomb-threatened London – brought the firm up to Chesterfield where it set up a factory, which helped the firm maintain a significant production schedule, providing both troops and those at home with much-needed sweet relief. Moreover, the firm's skills at managing relations with the government, and particularly the sweet ration, prepared the way for massive acquisition and expansion after the war. It was by no means plain sailing. Directors and staff worked hard and imaginatively to help the country's war effort. But unlike the nation as an economic force, the firm was not broken by the war. If anything, it was made by it.

Above: wartime restrictions on packaging materials meant many products were sold in simple wrapping.

War restrictions

Once war commenced, the confectionery industry became controlled by the Ministry of Food. This brought two major consequences: the Ministry rationed the allocation of raw materials to manufacturers and, secondly, it restricted sales and distribution to within regional zones to save fuel. Together these proved disastrous for some sweet firms. But fortunately for Robertson & Woodcock, the Ministry based each factory's sugar ration on what it had produced and sold in 1938/9 – a bumper year for the firm. Its ration was better than most.

The zoning arrangements divided England into north and south, only allowing companies to sell where they already had a business presence. Again, the firm was well placed. It had already been sending goods north to be sold by an agent called Mr Cramp. He agreed to be taken over by the firm, so enabling Trebor sweets to be sold throughout the war as far north as the Scottish border.

Early in 1939 the directors had already considered building a factory in the North. They had selected the Derbyshire town of Chesterfield, whose authorities claimed it to be within forty miles of a greater population of people than any other town in the country. On 25th July 1939 the board minutes reported plans for a £15,000 factory there. But by 13th September, with the arrival of war, the plans were shelved. The directors felt they should stick with their newly expanded facility at Forest Gate. But as the war progressed, a number of events forced them to reconsider.

> A quotation for 4-ounce bags of Wrapped Fruit Drops for the USA troops had been accepted at the price of 47/-d per gross and an order received for 8 tons. Management Report, 17th March 1943.

The firm's sugar ration was based on its output in 1938/9 – which was fortunately a bumper year.

The firm started to win special contracts for the War Office, the Admiralty and for NAAFI, which ran canteens and shops for the services. Later when American GIs started arriving, the firm was commissioned to provide them with *Extra-Strong Peppermints*. These government contracts stipulated that goods should be made outside danger areas. Forest Gate was not in the most dangerous spot for bombing, but anywhere in the centre or east of London was vulnerable. Moreover, much of the firm's machinery was from the Continent so fresh parts were out of reach. It was time to find a safer spot to make sweets.

Denis Hedley

During the late 1920s the Essex Regiment of the territorial army featured three subalterns who were not only to be become friends but also central to the firm. Two of them were Sydney J Marks and Cyril Robertson, both sons of founding partners. The third was Denis Hedley, who then worked as an electrical engineer with the Post Office.

In 1934 Hedley married Cyril Robertson's sister and headed off to work in Japan. Home on leave in 1936, he was persuaded by Sydney John to supervise construction of the new factory at Forest Gate. During the war Hedley commanded the 1st Bn, Essex Regiment and won the OBE for his service in France. He went on to become the firm's service manager, joining the board in 1950.

Denis Hedley

Chesterfield

Seeking a safer place to make sweets, far from enemy bombs, the firm found an old brewery in Derbyshire. Created within the chaos of wartime, the Chesterfield factory was to become one of Trebor's most important operations.

Hilda Clark *set up the Chesterfield factory and ran it for many years.*

In late 1940 the directors were desperate to find a quieter factory location. Though they had looked at Chesterfield before the war, the Derbyshire town was not their first priority – Robertson and Sidney Bonner, the firm's chief engineer, scouted widely around England for suitable premises. But then, early in 1941, the Chesterfield Brewery Company offered its disused brewery on lease. A decision was needed quickly, so key directors gathered from around the country to consider the premises. Colonel Sydney J Marks drove from the battalion he was commanding to pick up the chairman Mr Merrett in Lyme Regis then take him north to the site. Colonel Denis Hedley, the firm's sales manager, also had to cross the country from his posting. Bonner came up from London. They found a building that had been empty for eight years. 'It was completely gutted and looked like a ruined cathedral with a great rent in its roof,' wrote Bonner. But the chairman was insistent – 'the building would be worth buying for the bricks alone' he argued – and the board decided to lease it straightaway. Two months later it decided to purchase the site.

Bonner set about repairing the building. It needed new floors, but joists and girders were hard to come by during wartime in Derbyshire. So Bonner had material from bomb-damaged London buildings brought north; it was said that the upper floors were supported by old iron bedsteads.

Chesterfield: *the new factory backed onto green fields, but was handily next door to a railway station and goods yard. The firm soon made sure that everyone for miles around could see it was a Trebor factory.*

Meantime, the directors needed to find someone to run the Chesterfield operations. Many key staff were on army or territorial service, and Forest Gate was still running hard. They chose Hilda Clark who, since joining the company in 1918, had worked her way up to manage the sample room. Sydney J Marks later recalled her first sight of the site (see his memories alongside).

Clark set to work with two young girls as lorries from London started bringing up fifteen tons of goods a week for distribution to the midlands and north. Bonner filled the site with equipment from Forest Gate too valuable to be destroyed by German bombs. In Leeds he found a second-hand boiler which, with an assistant and some labourers, he manhandled into position. Manufacturing started on 9th April 1942 with a weekly target of five tons. This soon rose to ten tons. After Forest Gate was bombed in April 1944, production shifted north more rapidly, with over thirty four tons of manufacture transferred to Chesterfield within two months. This included both boilings and the newly named *Toffee Crunch*. (It couldn't be called *Toffee Butters* when there was no butter to be had.)

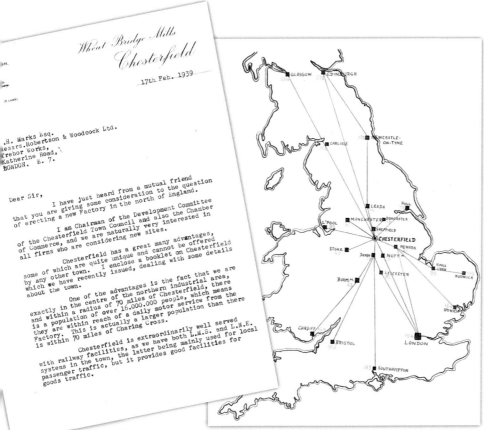

Sydney J Marks remembers

'It was Saturday 7th April 1941 that Mr Bonner driving an 8hp Standard, with Miss Clark, a tea chest filled with stationery, a typewriter perched on top, suitcases, hat boxes etc, called to collect me from an army course in Watford. On the way Mr Bonner told us of the tremendous difficulties he had had to get the ruins of the old Chesterfield Brewery waterproof and habitable. The three of us had dinner in this room, and Mr Bonner and I spent the rest of the evening trying to cheer up Miss Clark. We were living in rather trying times, she was leaving home for the first time, the job looked a bit much when she was closer up to it and she didn't know a soul in the place. On Sunday morning we took the tea chest over to the warehouse, helped her unpack it, showed her round the building, such as it was, a patched-up ruin; she was horrified. We showed her where to find the Labour Exchange, as it was called in those days, told her the job was all hers, wished her good luck and left her to it.'

Chesterfield's advantages

The Chesterfield authorities were keen to welcome Robertson & Woodcock as potential investors. The chairman of the town's development committee had already written in February 1939 (above) to extol the virtues of setting up a factory there.

He claimed that 16 million people lived within 70 miles of Chesterfield, a greater population than within the same radius of Charing Cross in London. Sat at the centre of England, the town not only lay within the northern industrial area, but was also well placed to serve all major British cities from one spot. Both the London Midland and the London & North Eastern Railways served the town, a crucial factor in these pre-motorway times.

The town clerk, a Mr Clegg, was a great help in setting up the operation. He even managed to find some local bedsteads to join those brought up from bomb-struck London. These served to hold together the new concrete put into the building.

The sweet ration

For eleven years from 1942 to 1953 the confectionery market was slimmed by rationing. Many children spent their entire childhood with sweets in short supply.

26th July 1942 saw the arrival of coupon books RB11 and RB11a, rationing sweets for adults and children alike. You could take your book to any shop-keeper who stocked sweets, chocolate or gum and they would snip out the requisite coupons for that four weekly period. The first ration was 2oz per person per week. Consumption before the war was 6.25oz per week so, at a stroke, the confectionery market was cut by two-thirds.

2oz was equivalent to just one *Mars Bar*. This worked in Trebor's favour as you could get a lot more pleasure from a coupon's worth of boiled sweets than a chocolate bar that disappeared in a few mouthfuls. In August 1942 the ration rose to 3oz. Prisoners of war were entitled to the same amount, which their relatives could buy and send them via the Red Cross. In 1949, after four years of peace, the ration had risen to 5.5oz. It finally ended in February 1953 in time for the coronation of Elizabeth II.

Wartime sweet wrappers offered little respite from the military mood of the time – but that was no doubt fine for the lucky children who managed to get their hands on some sweets. Paper and print restrictions meant packaging was mostly monochromatic but, as ever, the designers managed to pack plenty of action into their wrappers.

It was hard to design enticing wrappers when you had to highlight words like Points, Product Group and Controlled Price. Increasingly the firm sought to brand products with their own colour scheme, as demonstrated here by Frollies.

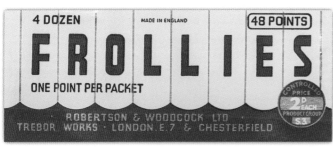

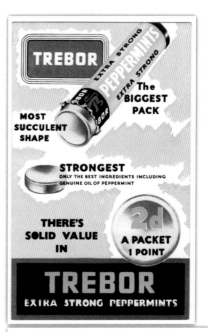

Wartime management

As if it weren't enough to have materials rationed, factories bombed, workers called up and operations controlled by the Ministry, the firm also had to cope with key directors away on war service.

Sydney J Marks spent much of the war travelling round the country – with postings in far-flung spots like the Orkney Islands, industry and government commitments in London and, when he could, his work for the firm.

Management of the firm changed, like so many things, during the war. Two board members were often absent on military service – Sydney J Marks and Cyril Robertson with the Essex Regiment of the Territorial Army. Service manager Denis Hedley won the OBE for service in France with the same regiment. To run the business and co-operate better with the Ministry, the directors appointed a managers' committee in May 1940. Along with the directors and Hedley, this included chief confectioner David Plaistowe, sales manager William Bitcheno, chief engineer Sidney Bonner and head buyer (later comptroller) Allan Hurndell. This committee proved effective. Indeed Trebor was lucky that key people like Bonner, Clark and Hurndell (for most of the war) were not called upon to fight.

It must have felt strange to have the firm's affairs regulated by the Ministry of Food. Even stranger, the industry now had to work together, negotiating with the government and sharing resources. The directors had always been active in the Cocoa, Chocolate and Confectionery Alliance. This Alliance assumed more significance than ever. As an example of co-operation, manufacturers now had to pool products for distribution around the county; so giving everyone access to lorries, and ensuring those lorries only travelled at full capacity.

Though Sydney J Marks was busy with his war service – spending much time commanding an anti-aircraft unit in the Orkney Islands north of Scotland – he carefully remained active in the Alliance. Watchful for opportunities and mindful of likely austerity when the war ended, he soon spotted how the firm might benefit from acquiring the sugar ration of small distributors.

The war also proved useful for recruitment: Marks found several key future managers of Trebor among the servicemen he led or served with, including Peter Kenyon, Sid Braithwaite, Alec Allen and Jack Weekes.

The Burma Baggers

Among many wartime contracts produced at Chesterfield was the 'Burma Contract.' This entailed making specially wrapped fruit-drops, to be parachuted down to the allied Chindit troops fighting the Japanese in the Burmese jungle. These drops contained ascorbic acid (Vitamin C) to help preserve health in such a difficult climate. Wrapping them was a specialised task, so the firm sent eight of its expert wrappers up from London. These young women arrived at midnight on a Saturday in April 1942, cold and exhausted, ready to start training Hilda Clark's local recruits on the Monday morning. They were well housed and looked after by local folk, who named the group the 'Burma Baggers'.

The bombs reach Forest Gate

In spring 1944 the luck ran out. For four years the factory at Forest Gate had avoided the horrors dropped upon East London by the German bombers, but now it received a direct hit. Luckily, few people were killed and the main factory was relatively untouched, but the severity of the damage was a serious shock to operations.

Below: the Forest Gate bomb scene shortly after the 1944 attack. Aside from repairing damage, it was crucial to secure the ruined factory against looters seeking sugar.

As the war progressed, the area around the factory at Forest Gate was one of few places in the East End to escape enemy air-raids. But the night of Tuesday 18th April 1944 brought the nightmare of a direct hit. As the factory caretaker Mr G Taylor reported, 'The building was severely damaged because the bomb landed in the warehouse and set fire to a great quantity of tea chests and tins of dry lemonade. A row of shops and houses across the way was destroyed by blast and through the heavy shutters of the garage being thrown across the street. Several people in the houses were killed, including one of the firm's stokers. But there was one miracle. For most of the war the firm had thrown open the basement to the public, and about two hundred of them were sheltering there that night. Imagine my relief on entering the basement to find not one casualty amongst them.' The board minutes reported, 'The office block was severely damaged by blast and fire and much valuable equipment was lost. As the offices were untenable, the staff and such equipment as was saved had to be moved to the Handwrapping Room in the Factory. Fortunately the Main Factory (apart from blast, damage to glass etc) was practically unhurt, and as soon as the water

connections were reconnected, production was started up immediately after only one week's delay.' On the same night Robert Robertson's home was severely damaged, so he and his wife moved up to Chesterfield. At one point during the war Sydney John also moved his family up to stay at the Portland Hotel in Chesterfield.

Fred Izard, who spent forty years in general maintenance at Forest Gate, later recalled cleaning up after the bomb. 'Number one boiling room suffered the most. We had to plug all the holes made by bomb splinters in the steam pipes and all the factory girls got to work chipping away the remaining glass fragments in the windows. It was one of the most wonderful sights – dozens of girls working away with little hammers and chisels. They cleared all the glass in two days.' One of the worst jobs was clearing shattered glass out of the big glucose tanks. Fred volunteered. 'They rigged up a bosun's chair over the tank. I put on a swimming costume and was lowered into the tank. Then I cut away the top layer of semi-solid glucose onto which the glass had fallen and put it into a bucket.' Several hours of sweaty work later, Fred was hauled out of the tank and had glucose removed from his bleeding legs.

The finishing off department at Chesterfield, where employees created final wrapping for gift boxes and other selections.

Mary Robertson (no relation to Robert Robertson) joined Trebor as personnel manager at the end of 1938. Her role was ground-breaking for such a firm.

'Sydney J Marks was the kingpin and he was way ahead of his time. He'd heard this (personnel work) was coming into fashion and he said to David Plaistowe, find somebody who will do this.'

Plaistowe found Robertson, then a lodger at his mother-in-law's boarding house in Dublin, invited her to London and offered her the job. She set about marshalling the growing army of women who worked in the newly expanded factory. 'I used to toddle around the factory finding out what kind of sweets they wanted to make. They were different every day, orders for this and orders for that, so we had to sort out how many workers they needed and where. Then I had the job of going to the foreman and saying, sorry they'll have to move machine. Nobody liked that; they preferred staying where they were. Back then there were heaps of jobs for unskilled girls in the East End of London. Getting them to stay was a constant headache.'

Summer was an uncomfortable time for making sweets. 'In hot weather it was dreadful - sticky, hot and smelly. One summer we took some lemonade on a trolley round the factory and gave glasses to the girls. I remember they put salt into the lemonade, though they didn't tell the girls, because they were losing such a lot in the heat. One hot, hot summer we allowed the girls to wear bathing suits or bikinis under their overalls, instead of dresses. That was a radical change and the girls appreciated it.'

New recruits were checked for standards of hygiene. 'We had this elderly nurse examine the girls before they came to be interviewed for work by me. If they had lice – and a great many did in those days – she had a secret code for letting me know so I did not offer them a job. One day I was sitting in my office and one of these enormous cockney women started shouting for me, banging the table and asking, why didn't you employ my Beryl? I was a bit scared, so I gave her a seat and a cup of tea, treated her like a duchess, and said, I'm sorry about your Beryl, but we make sweets in this factory and that means we must have cleanliness and unfortunately your Beryl has a dirty head. My Beryl may have a lice or two, she said, but she's not dirty. Luckily Mr Bonner helped me get her out of the factory.'

Wartime rationing brought temptations for those working in a sweet factory. 'When the war started, life became very tricky as sugar was rationed. We had a lot of people stealing sugar. They used to hide it in the gas masks we all had to carry. The directors decided to impose random searches at the gate as people left – anybody caught with sugar would be sacked on the spot. Unfortunately the first person they caught was a supervisor, an engineer or something. They couldn't afford to fire him, but they had to.'

Yet the company helped where it could. 'I had a diabetic cousin, a medical student in London, and he was in a terrible state of anxiety because he had to carry brown sugar on him for his diabetes – and he couldn't get it because of the war.' She made an official request – and Trebor gave her biscuit tins full of barley sugar for her cousin.

Working conditions

> It was suggested that "Music While You Work" be introduced and it was agreed to experiment with three half-hourly periods. The method of control was not decided upon. Management meeting, 25th February 1942

As war progressed, more workers were called up, including women later on. As with the First World War, the firm was prepared to pay any difference between service pay and Trebor pay, which helped offset some of the financial hardship, but this was not guaranteed for everyone. Those still with jobs had to work a lot harder. Every week was a six day week and, with the staff shortages and unexpected dilemmas raised by wartime, the pressures were great – and given the suffering of so many, it was no time to complain. Nevertheless, Sydney J Marks knew that productivity depended on a happy workforce; as often as he could visit the factories from his war work in Orkney, he gave motivational speeches. In 1944 the firm launched the Trebor Provident Fund, including cover for death by enemy action. The next year it introduced an Employee Profit Sharing Scheme.

Extreme wartime conditions made people think about productivity. As personnel manager Mary Robertson explained,

> *'The thing that triggered the whole thing off was the shocking hours that the early munitions workers worked in the first world war. Somebody came up with the brilliant idea that if you shortened the hours, you would not get less work – you would actually get more.'*

In March 1945 the directors invited the consultancy Public Administration (PA) into Forest Gate to see how workers could be helped to become more efficient. Then, as now, one of the country's largest consulting firms, PA recommended better training and communication between management and workers. They also warned of a 'yes man' culture and noted that managers tended to shirk decisions on even trivial matters if they feared the boss might disagree with them. Sydney John approved their proposals, put Cyril Robertson in charge and soon PA was flooding Forest Gate with studies of time & motion studies, personnel performance and machine capability. Trebor was adjusting to peacetime.

Bill Deighan remembers

'I remember reading a story about a young girl who gave her boyfriend a few sweets from the factory. He was a fireman, this was during the war, and he was caught going up East Ham High Street by a policeman who found he'd got sweets on him. So he was taken in, charged with theft and fined about fifteen pounds. This was a time when bombs were falling on the East End and you couldn't walk up the High Street for shrapnel and anti aircraft guns – and yet this guy has been caught with a few sweets.'

Sydney H Marks dies

On 27th February 1941, amidst the frenzy of planning a move north to Chesterfield, the firm lost the man whose energy and forward thinking did so much to create the business back in the early 1900s and whose family were to steer that business through much of the century. Sydney Herbert Marks died.

He was later remembered by Elizabeth Cornford, who had joined the firm in 1920 as a clerk: 'He was a wonderful man to work for, and there was never a dull moment as he was very energetic and had a great sense of humour. He thought nothing of arriving at seven o'clock in the morning, working all day and giving a hand over anything. Under his enthusiasm we all enjoyed the excitement of turning from one job to another as long as our sweets were delivered to the customers.'

TREBOR SWEETS
OBERTSON & WOODCOCK LTD
facturing Confectioners
ON & CHESTERFIELD
KRA 74 E

POST-WAR BOOM

Trebor greeted peacetime at full speed. Despite the rigours of rationing, the firm grew fast by staying agile, building new plant and, most importantly, buying up other businesses.

Adjusting to peace

Wartime had taught the directors that buying other businesses, and their ration allocation, was a good way to grow. The firm now embarked on an acquisition spree to harness the opportunities of peacetime.

On 14th August 1945 the board gathered for an important meeting. Japan would still fight for one more day, but hostilities had ended in Europe three months earlier. Since then Sydney Marks had been planning how the firm might profit from peacetime and now, on this sunny summer Tuesday, he presented his ideas to the directors. These proposals, warmly approved by the board, were central to the firm's future success, so it is worth quoting his plan from the minutes:

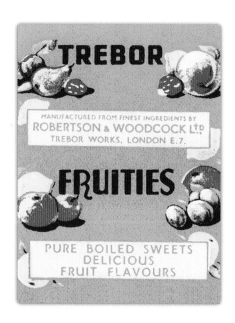

> **'Acquisition of other Firms in the Trade to increase the total production of the Company, either by purchase outright or acquiring a controlling interest.'**

Over the next fifteen years, Trebor was to buy up the manufacturing and wholesaling capacity of tens of smaller firms.

> **'That the introduction of Count Items in lieu of weight lines would increase the selling price by a figure estimated to be £38 per ton. These count lines were in course of preparation and when fully in production would increase turnover by around £26,000 per annum.'**

Buying a chosen weight of sweets, measured out by the shopkeeper from glass jars, was in decline. There was more profit in countlines – products that were individually packaged and priced – which also showed that adults were eating more sweets.

> **'To register and protect the word Trebor and to utilise the Company to promote the sale of the Company's products under the Trade Mark Trebor.'**

As the wholesale of other firm's products became less important to the firm, so Trebor should come to the fore.

> **'Export Trade: That the Company should explore the possibilities of establishing factories in the Colonies and Foreign Countries, and that an experiment might be made in Denmark where the firm traded before the war and from whence the firm's agent Mr Pedersen has enquired the prospects of re-opening business.'**

Overseas expansion was to be one of the most exciting Trebor stories of the post-war decades.

> **'Employees' Bonus Scheme. Resolved that in order to bring the Title of the Scheme into one which more correctly describes its purpose the name should be changed to The Trebor Profit Sharing Scheme.'**

Finding imaginative ways to improve the welfare of workers was to become a central ambition of the firm.

'Appointment of Miss H. M. Clark to the Board of Managers in consideration of her services as manageress of the Chesterfield Factory over the past three years.'

Hilda Clark had received her 25 Years Service gold watch the previous year. Her work at Chesterfield was crucial to Trebor's war effort. Her success showed how the war enabled some women to punch through the glass ceiling of industry.

Against most of these action points, Mr S J Marks was the person directed to investigate and proceed. Sydney was now clearly the main force within the firm. His father had died in 1941 and his brother Alex concentrated on the firm's fleet of lorries. With Woodcock dead and King now 80 and far into retirement, Robert Robertson was the only founding director still attending board meetings, but he no longer took the lead; his son Cyril Robertson took three months leave from the Army in September 1945 to work with the consultants Personal Administration (PA) as they investigated the firm's factory methods. He, too, seemed content with a subsidiary role. This left Sydney in charge.

Peter Kenyon arrives

In April 1943 the firm bought Bennington Park Farm near Stevenage in Hertfordshire. The farm served various purposes: it supplied milk for making toffee; its vegetables and milk helped the factory canteen; and it was intended at one point to be used for advertising. But it also helped persuade Peter Kenyon to join as production manager at Forest Gate in 1949. Sydney Marks had got to know Kenyon during the war; years later Marks tracked him down to Darlington, where he was working in a wool factory and from where his wife needed persuading to move south.

'Sydney knew he would need to win over my wife Margaret if he had any hope of me taking the job,' Kenyon later explained.' He persuaded Margaret, before I had even seen the factory, to go and have a look. She got on the train at Darlington; she got off at Hatfield and was met by Sydney and Muriel, his wife. They took her to lunch, then to the works and then round possible places where we could live. Finally to a Queen Anne farmhouse in Hertfordshire. He offered to make the first floor into a flat and

this settled the matter for my wife.' Private motor cars were still hard to come by in 1949 – and the farm was a fair distance from town – so Kenyon commuted to Forest Gate at 7am each morning in a company van, bringing in the farm's milk and vegetables. Once again Marks used his ingenuity to make a key appointment. The farm was sold in 1951, but gave rise to an interesting board minute of 11th June 1946:

Farm affairs: S J Marks reported that the following animals had been entered at Chelmsford Show: Barnes Daisy (Reserve Silver Medal Best Cow), Muirlaugh Lucille (3rd prize in Calf Cow) & Barnes Canty.

Peter Kenyon

Jack Weekes remembers

During the hard winter of 1947 a young man arrived at Chesterfield. He had already survived the tough training process at Forest Gate, when Sydney Marks once looked at his hands and asked 'Where are your blisters?' His name was Jack Weekes and he had served under Marks' command during four years of war. Weekes' impressions of the factory were mixed. 'I remember it was derelict in places and where the canteen is today was a yard full of old tyres and coal-heaps. In an adjacent building was an office for the town's Clerk of the Court – the court was then across the way. The first floor was the production floor – the top floor was for storage and a couple of gas-fires were used for making Crystal Mints and Crystal Barley.' Within a few years, the Chesterfield factory employed over 700 people. Weekes started there as production manager but was destined to become Trebor's chief confectioner.

Growing the business

Cleverly deploying the ration rules enabled Trebor to maintain production levels. Purchasing other firms enabled it to increase them.

Although war was over, the firm's factories still cried out for sugar and glucose. Until rationing ended in September 1953, supply of these raw materials got even tighter, while the firm became cannier at bypassing regulations. For example, while glucose was rationed, apple syrup was not. Working with the loyal Mr Pedersen in Denmark, chief buyer Allan Hurndell arranged for water (and a few peeled apples) to be added to glucose, then imported to England under the label of syrup. An Austrian refugee chemist called Forster calculated the exact proportion of water to glucose that would suit the machines. As a result, the firm enjoyed far greater supply of glucose than it was supposed to receive.

Sugar proved trickier. As John Marks explained, 'Hurndell went to bed with the regulations and realised you could import spa water in whatever quantity you wished – it wasn't rationed. Spa Water was defined as containing trace elements, but there was no restriction on how much sugar might be included. So we asked the Danes to put in as much sugar as the liquid could hold at room temperature – around two thirds of the volume.' The "spa water" duly arrived in London by the barrel, but a major challenge remained. As Clifford Broom remembered, 'We bought this stuff in but the thing we desperately wanted was dry sugar, not syrup. Peter Kenyon spoke to Fred Nicholls the foreman, a wonderful confectioner, and he said to Fred, if we put this syrup in a pan and boil it we should get sugar shouldn't we? Yes I suppose so, said Fred, but we may end up with a lump of sugar, not powder. So they got a pan organised, put in the spa water, waited for the water to disappear, then they opened it up and Fred said, bloody hell, look, there's sugar powder lying at the bottom.'

Sydney Marks was very proud of this technical ingenuity. Undoubtedly the firm was sailing close to the wind, but this was probably essential for any business seeking to survive, let alone prosper, in such times of austerity.

Growth by acquisition

Another way to acquire ration was to buy companies who held it. During the war, the firm had learnt how to make use of other companies' allocation. The Confectionery Alliance had persuaded the government to distinguish between raw materials

Celebration: *there was no ration on the sugar used to celebrate the Chesterfield factory with this 1952 cake.*

Left: *when the firm acquired a wholesaler, it usually retained the trading name, while using company vans for promoting Trebor products. Later on, many of these businesses would be gathered within the Moffat wholesale umbrella.*

and half-finished goods, so enabling Trebor to buy up the sugar ration of smaller firms in return for semi-processed sweets for packing under their own names.

John Marks explained the thinking behind this. 'A lot of wholesalers of all sorts of confectionery used to have a little bit of sweet making on the side. Those who were really clever would buy our unwrapped sweets, wrap them and sell them for a penny more a quarter, which was less than the cost of wrapping them under their own name. This meant they had allocations of sugar, but to make a ton of sweets a week was a palaver – so we went around buying their allocations of sugar so that we could add to our production. That led us to realise we could increase our share of the market by buying the actual wholesaling company and sell our sweets through them.'

'Acquisition of D.G. Embling, Newport, 20.3 Tons per annum. Acquisition of D. Scott, Abergavenny, 15 Tons per annum.' Minutes 1st December 1949

Bristol Sweets Ltd was one of the first companies to be purchased, in November 1945. Thereafter the board minutes became littered with details of new takeovers: in the period up to 1960 Trebor was to acquire fifty or so smaller firms, swiftly incorporating their sugar allocation, machinery and product brands.

Fifties Sales Conference: *Thursday 11th February 1954 saw a gathering of all Trebor's sales representatives, plus the great and good of the firm, at Clacton's Grosvenor Court Hotel. By Saturday night they were ready to party and Sydney Marks took part in the 'Cafe Crunchinental' after dinner entertainment. Seen here in the front row, starting fourth from left: Hilda Clark, Denis Hedley, Sydney Marks, Robert Robertson, Cyril Robertson, Alex Marks, Sidney Bonner and Allan Hurndell.*

Woodford and Trebor House

Further out in East London arose a new factory and the firm's first headquarters building.

In May 1949 the firm started negotiations to buy some property in Woodford Avenue, Ilford. Sidney Bonner had been looking out for somewhere to expand production in East London as Forest Gate was already full to capacity. He found a disused coachworks five miles further out in the eastern suburbs, with a large bungalow and garden offering room for expansion. Once it was purchased, Cyril Robertson took charge of converting the coachworks into a sweet factory; this was not easy as it had been used to make tank shells during the war. The firm brought there its production of compressed sugar goods such as *Extra Strong Mints* and *Refreshers*.

Behind the Woodford factory the firm built a warehouse in 1954 to handle export packing and despatch. The newly emerging customers from Lagos and Baghdad, Hong Kong and Toronto may have liked the same sweets as the good people of London and Manchester, but they needed them packaged differently. At the same time it was far too expensive to export the goods in glass jars. This warehouse specialised in serving each market in the way it demanded.

Later in 1956, on the site of the bungalow, a brand new headquarters arose – bursting with all the modern style of the time – which was aptly named Trebor House just like the first premises back in 1907. This provided offices for the directors and managers, along with space for the fast-growing administration staff.

Right: Sydney Marks addresses the first profit share meeting in July 1951. He's standing on the terrace of the old tennis pavilion which then existed at the back of the lot.

Woodford – built for compressed sweets

The new factory on Woodford Avenue, Ilford, started operations in 1949 and was the first British factory to be devoted entirely to compressed sugar goods. Back in 1929, with state-of-the-art equipment from Germany, the firm pioneered the creation of such sweets in the UK. This involved milling granulated sugar, blending it into a flavoured dough and then compressing it into tablet form. The result was peppermints and other popular products such as *Refreshers*. Not only was manufacture largely mechanical; so was wrapping and packaging.

Woodford factory: this 1949-50 photo shows the recently converted coachworks. The grassy area behind the factory later became an export warehouse, while Trebor House was built partly on top of the next door bungalow and its swimming pool.

Alf Dixon, factory manager at Woodford from the early 1950s, later recalled:
'The factory started up with two Hartmann and Stein roll-wrappers on which we wrapped round tablets embossed with the name Trebor. We also had two wrappers for square *Refresher*-type sweets called *Frubes* and *Fizzets*, and two more machines for wrapping rectangular mints for export to Nigeria under the brand name *Peerless Mints*.

'The sugar was delivered from Tate & Lyle in two hundredweight hessian sacks, to be tipped into the sugar mills. In those days the sugar mills were always exploding and dried powder was piled up in half-hundredweight sacks, which had to be manually tipped into the mixers for damping down and flavouring. We made about eighty to ninety tons a week. Brian Jarvis was king of the export warehouse – he was an expert at strapping and stencilling the huge wooden cartons we used for sending tins of toffee and peppermints abroad.'

Refreshers were one of Woodford's most popular products.

Trebor House

In March 1956 the firm's management and administrative staff moved into the new Trebor House. Built alongside the Woodford Factory in East London, this remained the firm's headquarters until the sale to Cadbury in 1989. In 1979 the firm upgraded the building with a complete new top floor.

The boardroom (below) and reception (left) reflected the modern design stylings of the mid 1950s.

Arthur Sansome remembers

'Before the war, confectionery was entirely a craft industry. The foremen had their secret recipes and were kings in their own little area. After the war, when the market expanded and we started doing export, we had to bring in technical people, professional engineers and chemists, rather than people who just learned on the job. So it changed from being a craft industry to a chemical engineering material handling industry. No more chief confectioner, but plenty of food technologists.'

Right: Cyril Robertson (seen here in 1970) was the son of Robert Robertson, one of the four founders of the firm. He served with Sydney J Marks and Denis Hedley in the same Territorial Army battalion before joining the board in 1931. Thereafter he took several roles with the firm including, in 1949, overseeing the development of the Woodford factory.

Forest Gate in the late 1940s

Following the bomb damage of 1944, the art deco factory (below right) was painted white with the distinctive TREBOR QUALITY SWEETS lettering which exists to this day. Centre left you can see Trebor Terrace, the original houses built in 1894. Behind the factory is the schoolyard of Shaftesbury Road Primary School into which Hilda Clark threw sweets to celebrate Armistice Day in 1918. The handsome brick chimney remains a prominent local landmark to this day; back when the factory was active, its entire stack was coated in linseed every few years to weatherproof the brickwork. In 2003 the factory was converted into 51 loft-style flats.

Above: Harry Barber boils Crystal Mints on a gas-fired pan in No. 3 Boiling Room at Forest Gate around 1950. Such tiny batches were soon a thing of the past.

Right: some processes defied mechanisation, such as interlocking the strips that made up Bullseyes.

Left: Clifford Broom joined the company in 1949 and took responsibility for manufacturing at Forest Gate and Woodford in 1957.

FACTORY NOTICE No 218
JANUARY 1949

Clogs must not be worn while playing Table Tennis

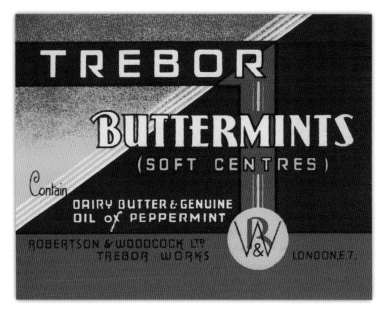

Individuality: for most of the twentieth century each product had its own personality and look. Though the word Trebor became more prominent in the 1950s, with a similar-ish typeface, the dull grip of modern branding – with its demand for conformity to a single range-wide style – was still many years away.

Above: *The Trebor Times helped the firm keep contact with retailers, even if it did not supply them directly.*

Right: *Sydney Marks' daughter Diana, a student at London's St Martin's School of Arts, painted these murals in the Chesterfield canteen during the early 1950s.*

Alex Marks, pictured left in 1955, was Sydney H Marks' other son. He joined the firm in 1920 and became a director in 1929. Over the years he took a number of roles, working as a buyer, salesman, transport manager and production controller. He also took an interest in training and personnel matters. Alex and Sydney had a sister, Stella, who became very involved with the Barnardo's charity for children.

Above: a smart new fleet of Trebor vans and liveried drivers lines up during the 1950s.

Do sweets harm teeth? Heck no, say doctors

As rationing ended, and many people felt austerity had actually made them healthier, so some asked whether sweets promote tooth decay. Fortunately for the industry, the Medical Research Council (MRC) came out on their side. Reporting in the *Lancet* about a research project in which children were repeatedly fed sweets then sent to bed without cleaning their teeth, the MRC claimed, 'You can break your tooth on a bullseye. You can pull out a filling with some toffee. But to suggest that sugar is in contact with teeth for long enough to cause decay is pure nonsense.' Doctors would not always prove to be so supportive, but Trebor keenly fought its corner: a 1981 staff magazine pointed out that UK consumers ate far more sweets per head than most other western countries, but suffered less tooth decay per head, so 'other factors must be more significant'.

Chesterfield at work and play

Post-war Britain saw less divide between work and home than today. People worked longer hours and were happy to socialise with their colleagues. Even company spirit was a credible force. These photos from Chesterfield factory during the 1950s show some of the ways staff worked and played together.

UNLOADING SUGAR (above): Brenda Ashley empties a huge bag of sugar. Aged 18 she joined the Chesterfield factory when it opened during the war. 43 years of continuous service later, she had a big retirement party in 1986.

HAND WRAPPING (right): although there were machines to wrap most count lines, specialty sweets and boxed assortments demanded wrapping by hand.

WASHING JARS (below): some days the firm might have 10,000 glass jars to wash.

COLOURING AND FLAVOURING (above): well before the 1950s the laboratory had taken control of production, with chemists prescribing the colours and flavours to be added, as here, on the slab.

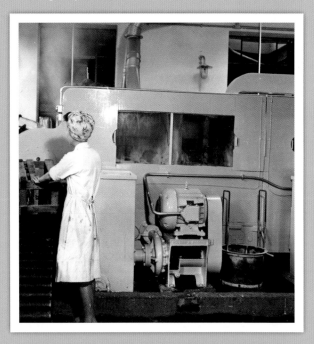

LOADING THE BATCH ROLLER (left): once a batch had been worked by hand to mix in the colour and flavouring, it was time to roll it out to consistent width.

WEIGHING UP: though count lines of individual products were increasing, most sweets were still sold by weight.

THE LOADING BAY: set at the heart of England, Chesterfield was well placed for sending out liveried vans across the nation.

CHRISTMAS DINNER: on 20th December 1955 the works canteen echoed to the sound of workers belting out traditional carols.

POULSBROOK TIGERS (below): pictured in 1955, this women's football team was active in Chesterfield factory's social club, playing to raise money for local retirement homes. For many working class women of the time, there were few opportunities to play sport outside what their employer might offer.

CHESTERFIELD CRICKET TEAM: the first outing of this amateur eleven on 25th June 1956 saw them dismissed for 30 runs by a local team, one of whom 'had appeared for the county seconds.' But they improved, beating another local team on 21st July with five wickets to spare.

SPORTS DAY 1959: Sydney Marks encourages the foremen in their tug of war against the warehousemen. The foremen won with two straight pulls.

Unlocking the world

After the interruptions of war, it was time for Trebor to look abroad for fresh markets.

Looking back in 1971, Sydney Marks wrote, 'one of the stupidest government decisions of the early post-war years was the decision not to take sugar as part of Marshall Aid.' He was referring to the multi-billion dollar support given by the United States to rebuild Western Europe after the war. 'Holland had no such scruples,' he continued, 'and was to build up her export trade very substantially as a result. We could have bought sugar at world prices with American aid. Instead the ludicrous situation arose where British manufacturers were buying cases of fondant and other mixtures with high sugar contents and re-processing them. The result was that many of our competitors on the continent obtained considerable benefits at the expense of British consumers.'

Sydney had long had his eye on overseas markets. Ever since he first visited German sweet manufacturers in the 1920s, he knew technical expertise was greater across the Channel. But there were further barriers of entry for British sweetmakers. Many continental companies enjoyed government subsidy, while currency conditions and other commercial restrictions made trade difficult with countries like France and Belgium. As late as 1947 the British government forbade firms from exporting more than they had done before the war. But in northern Europe, thanks to its old ally Thorvald Pedersen in Copenhagen, the firm set up the Trebor Candy Company and started making inroads into Scandinavia; Sweden was to be particularly successful during this period.

These sales helped raise the sugar quota back home while rationing continued. As Sydney Marks later recalled, 'For every ton of sweets we sold export, we were

Bill Lettington: *when Trebor's first export manager joined in 1935 from Crosse & Blackwell, he had only three customers to serve. When he retired two decades later, the firm's export tonnage was among the industry's greatest.*

Below left: *seen in 1957, staff from the distribution warehouse get crates of peppermints ready for their journey to Penang, Malaysia.* **Below:** *Kingsway Stores in Lagos was the scene for a Trebor sales drive in the autumn of 1956. Though the Nigerian government had recently increased the import duty on sweets to 50% of value, West Africa was to become one of the firm's main export markets.*

permitted to buy an extra ton of sugar to produce goods for sale in the home market. All eyes were on the export department – how to get more orders, how to get the goods to their destinations quicker. This was Arthur Franks' job. Save a week on each order to a customer, then we might get an extra order or two a year'. Arthur Franks went on to become director of Trebor Overseas and in 1977 was awarded an OBE for services to export.

During the early 1950s Trebor tried to crack North America. It set up companies called Trebor Confections in Canada in 1950 and in the US in 1952, each with their own sales organisations. Neither experiment worked, so the firm resorted to working through agents. Soon Canada alone represented 20% of all exports, while US sales grew well through both department stores and sales agents.

Elsewhere, the remnants of the British Empire proved fertile to Trebor during the 1950s. Consumers in Malaya, Nigeria and the West Indies loved its sweets, as did people around the Middle East, particularly in Iraq, Kuwait and Bahrein. When the company's first export manager Bill Lettington retired in 1955, he must have been proud at the way his department had reached out from

ration-ravaged Britain to serve the world. At that time confectionery was the third largest food export from Britain, after whisky and refined sugar, and Trebor contributed well to the success. The company then claimed its sweets to be reaching every market where they were allowed to be imported. But this was just the start. The 1960s were to see remarkable leaps in Trebor's overseas record, with the company and Sydney Marks recognised as one of the nation's greatest exporters.

Arthur Franks: *Trebor's overseas director, he received the OBE for services to export.*

Right: inside this 1950s Export Catalogue, products like Old English Mint Humbugs (below) were packaged traditionally for overseas customers. Extra Strong Peppermints were popular in tropical climates.

TREBOR OLD ENGLISH MINT HUMBUGS

Traditional English peppermint boiled sweets.

Golden Jubilee

The firm always liked to celebrate. So when its 50th birthday came along, there were lavish parties in London and Chesterfield, along with a jubilant brochure and twelve months of joyful events.

'The Royal Festival Hall was filled on Tuesday night when 1,800 employees of Robertson and Woodcock, Ltd., were the guests of the board of directors at the company's Golden Jubilee party.'

So read the *Express & Independent* newspaper on 25th January 1957. It was quite a party: dancing to Nat Temple and his band, a tableau of Trebor employees dressed up in costumes from the past half century, cabaret from Ted Ray and The Dazzles dancing girls, 500 balloons released at midnight, plus fleets of buses to take everyone home. Robert Robertson, the grand old man of the firm, was applauded for kissing his wife as he ended his speech. Sydney Marks thanked all the loyal and enthusiastic 'Treborites', praised the Trebor Spirit, but couldn't resist making gentle digs at the honoured guests, the Mayors of Woodford and East Ham, for their 'unsympathetic officials.'

Racier than the press report was the description of the party in The Trebor Magazine: 'The party had everything; now brilliant, now tender; now gay; now moving; now riotous; now thoughtful. One's own thoughts moved in step. Now rockin' and rollin' with the young and the future; now waltzing with the old and the past; now at the quick-step with those whose powers are at their height today.'

The firm was clearly determined to celebrate its 50th birthday in style. Aside from the London party, it had hosted a big do two weeks earlier at Sheffield's Cutlers' Hall for the Chesterfield staff. There's a picture from The Derbyshire

Jubilee Top Table: the firm's 50th anniversary was celebrated in grand style at a party for Chesterfield employees at the Cutler's Hall, Sheffield on 10th January 1957. Here seen behind the lobsters and Trebor-shaped cakes on the top table were (from left): Wenna Simpson and John Marks (to be married three months later), Angela Marks (married to Ian), Mrs Alex Marks, Ian Marks, Mrs C Robertson, Mrs Hedley, Cyril Robertson, Robert Robertson, Alex Marks, Hilda Clark, Clive Robertson, Sydney Marks, Denis Hedley and Sydney's wife Muriel Marks.

Times of this event, showing all the directors and key family members lined up behind a series of cakes spelling out the firm's name.

Proud of its history, the firm produced a lavish Golden Jubilee Brochure – a snapshot of a forward-thinking firm, which extolled its past, but prized its modernity and place in the world. 'We have tried to keep a family feeling in the organisation, which at its best is a feeling of warmth and security,' wrote Sydney Marks in the foreword, going on to say, 'Trebor has exported far more than most and even if this has not always been as profitable as the home market we have, in our small way, helped our country to obtain foreign currency and to show that Trebor quality means that to buy British is to buy wisely.'

In a long section headed How Our Products Are Made, the brochure praises the company's increasing mechanisation of production, its use of air conditioning and its 'all-seeing eye', an electromagnetic detector for spotting tiny pieces of metal which had got into the mix. Pictures show a clinically-clean working environment, where gloved and hatted staff monitor machines to wash bottles, sort boiled sweets or wrap mints.

A map of Trebor's World Markets resembles a map of the British Empire, along with countries such as the USA, Italy and Sweden. 'We can quote the hundreds of tons of TREBOR sweets sold each year in small fancy tins of special designs which, probably not acceptable in the United Kingdom, are received eagerly by Arab and Chinese customers in Baghdad, Mosul, Kuala Lumpur and Hong Kong. We can quote *Wappi* caramels in the Gold Coast, the multi-sized polythene packs in the U.S.A. and Canada, and the special Red and Gold for Chinese markets, where Blue is a sign of mourning and completely foreign to the joy and festivity which surrounds the buying of confectionery.' The importance of Scandinavia is shown by the choice of only two foreign partners to be featured: Thorvald Pedersen and Sven Jacobsen of Denmark.

Sydney and his wife Muriel arrive at the Royal Festival Hall in London for the 50th Anniversary party in January 1957.

C A Fletcher remembers

'Let our minds go back to a day early in 1907 and picture a few individuals gathered to witness the erection of a small brick stove, on which was to rest a large iron slab with a hole in its centre to hold a copper boiling pan. Slab tables were erected and the rest of the equipment for making boiled sweets consisted of a few hand rollers. The premises comprised a small building with stables standing in the ground at the back of the houses. It was a very modest start. But there was one great advantage – the men who set the rollers in motion possessed great skill in the sweet trade.'

Jubilee brochure

Created for the firm's 50th birthday, this snapshot of Trebor in 1957 tells a proud tale of technical innovation, marketing might and global ambition.

TREBOR

GOLDEN JUBILEE

1957

ROBERTSON & WOODCOCK LIMITED

BOARD OF DIRECTORS

R. ROBERTSON
Director and Secretary
4th January, 1907

The late S. H. MARKS,
Director, 4th January, 1907
Managing Director, 28th March, 1908
Chairman, 25th July, 1933

S. J. MARKS, T.D.,
Director,
24th February, 1932
Vice-Chairman, 1956

H. C. MERRETT, F.C.A.,
Director,
11th June, 1936
Chairman, 7th February, 1941

E. A. MARKS,
Director,
23rd July, 1928

C. R. ROBERTSON, T.D.,
Director,
26th January, 1930

A. G. DENNIS, LL.M.,
Director,
19th March, 1953

D. J. HEDLEY, O.B.E., T.D.,
Director,
26th January, 1950

It is with a sense of pride and humility that I am pre[...]
50th Anniversary brochure with the hope that you may find [...]
interest.

We tell you of fifty years of endeavour, of growth from small[...]
of the constant search for technical improvements, of the consta[...]
quality, to ensure that the customer eats the best that money c[...]
at a price within reach of all pockets including the children's.

We have tried to keep a family feeling in the organisation, [...]
best is a feeling of warmth and security.

We are happy to record our acute awareness of the fact that [...]
success is due to a loyal and enthusiastic staff whose enterprise a[...]
over a long period has done so much to support and encourage[...]
who have been entrusted with the management of the company.

We have always received great help from our customers an[...]
many of whom have been our friends for longer than I care to r[...]
without whom our progress would not have been possible.

Trebor has exported far more than most and even if this ha[...]
been as profitable as the home market we have, in our small way[...]
country to obtain foreign currency and to show that Trebor q[...]
that to buy British is to buy wisely.

We look forward to the new generation now beginning to tak[...]
our organisation, not only continuing old traditions but constantly infusing
new ideas and methods into the business, auguring well for a bigger and
better Trebor in the years to come.

Sydney J Marks

SALES FORCE PERSONALITIES

D. W. JARVIS,
Representative, 1922
Area Manager, 1950

F. R. BOYDEN,
Representative, 1946
Export Representative, 1947
Export Manager, 1954
Sales Manager, 1955

H. P. de ROEPER, D.S.M., T.D.,
Asst. London Area Manager, 1937
Area Manager, 1945

S. M. HOWELL,
Representative, 1937
Area Manager, 1955

K. C. HOWELL,
Representative, 1935
Area Manager, 1955

D. C. HUMPHREY,
Representative, 1946
Area Manager, 1953

G. I. REID,
Representative, 1950
Area Manager, 1955

J. C. FINDLAY,
Representative, 1951
Area Manager, 1955

F. G. FARMAN,
Export Representative, 1955
Export Manager, 1955

D. T. BAILEY,
Representative, 1953
Area Manager, 1955

Left and right: when it first appeared at the 1954 Motor Show at London's Earls Court, the Trebor Mobile Showroom demonstrated the skills of British motor manufacture. It also reflected the sophistication of the firm's wholesale activities. No wonder Trebor displayed it proudly in the 1957 Jubilee Brochure.

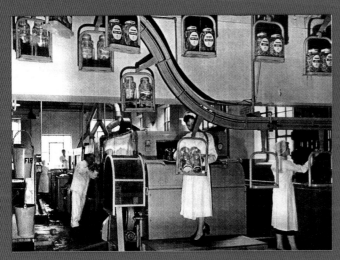

Left: *Chesterfield's futuristic machinery for washing jars.*

Below: *the world and its ingredients, seen through the eyes of the 1950s.*

ALEX·P·PACKHAM

Origin of Contents

TREBOR
QUALITY
SWEETS

CORNFLOUR

MAIZE FOR GLUCOSE

PEPPERMINT OIL

SALT

BEET SUGAR

CONDENSED MILK

LIME OIL

CANE SUGARS

COCOA

TARTARIC ACID

CITRIC ACID

LEMON AND ORANGE OILS

VEGETABLE FATS

William Bitcheno remembers

'I joined the Trebor selling staff in 1924 with a London territory and, armed with a couple of sample bags, I sallied forth into the unknown. For 12 months or so I found the going rather difficult, but the directors showed me every encouragement and the customers were very helpful as I gained their confidence. I was appointed London sales manager in 1931 and – much earlier in my career than I could have anticipated even in my wildest dreams – sales manager in 1938.

'Vivid in my mind are the sales staff conferences which were held fortnightly and directed by the late Mr S. H. Marks. On these occasions travellers were kept in close touch with process developments and the general progress of the Company and were able to express their opinions on the constant flow of new lines. It was the personality of the late Mr Marks, however, that illuminated the proceedings. The sales staff owe a deep debt of gratitude to him for the experienced guidance he was able to give in his genial humorous way.' From the 1957 brochure.

1958–1969

GOING
GLOBAL

This decade was book-ended by the acquisitions of two famous sweet firms: Sharps Toffees in 1961 and Clarnico in 1969. Meanwhile Trebor became recognised as one of the nation's great exporters.

Into the 60s

As the firm lost its founder Robert Robertson, a new generation of Marks came on board.

In 1958 Sydney's two sons John and Ian were appointed to the board. Born in 1930, John had gone to Cambridge then worked in the United States before coming to work full-time for the firm in 1953. Ian, three years younger, also went to Cambridge then spent six months at the Hansella factory in Germany for his 'apprenticeship' before joining the firm. Now as directors in 1958, John headed off to explore the Australian market and Ian started work as production controller.

While Sydney Marks remained firmly in charge, the Old Guard were changing. At the end of the 1950s ill health forced Merrett to hand over chairmanship to Robertson, himself very elderly. Then in November 1961 Robertson died. Aged 84, he had spent 54 years with the company he co-founded; indeed he kept an office in Trebor House until a few months before he died. In the same year Hilda Clark, the steely Eastender who'd left London to set up the Chesterfield operation during the midst of the war, retired as divisional manager. Among the New Guard were a triumvirate of advisers for Sydney: accountant Clyde Dixie, solicitor Kevin Kennedy and accountant Arthur Kearns, who joined the firm via its acquisition of Moffat in Manchester.

A major British company

By now Robertson & Woodcock was a major British company with thousands of employees. This size demanded new systems, so the firm was reorganised into eight divisions: Executive, Buying, Sales, Forest Gate and Woodford Factories, Chesterfield Factory, Engineering, Training and Accounting.

Back in 1956 chief engineer Sidney Bonner and chief confectioner Jack Weekes went to Germany on one of the firm's periodic trawls for new technology. This time they discovered Hansella's new Uniplast forming machine and promptly ordered one for Chesterfield. This, plus other developments, enabled the firm to enter new sectors of the sweet market with, for example, chocolate-centred rolls branded *Sonnets*. A new line of sour fruits called *Regal Crown* did particularly well in the United States, so raising export tonnage considerably.

Having survived the shortages of the 1950s, Trebor was well placed to ride the wave of industrial optimism washed in by the 1960s. Sugar prices fell. Production shifted from the old batch method to continuous production. New machines allowed faster wrapping and handling of finished

In Memoriam

The announcement of the death of Mr. Robert Robertson, the Chairman of Robertson and Woodcock Ltd., on Friday, the 3rd November, was received with the deepest regret throughout the entire Trebor organisation.

He was the last surviving founder director of the firm; his surname is incorporated in the title of the company he helped to found in 1907 and his Christian name reversed is the trademark TREBOR.

Trebor, to him, conveyed the spirit of the organisation he helped to create. Starting in Shaftesbury Road, Forest Gate, London, his early interests were in the accountancy field but in 1918 he became responsible for production and did great work during the next decade to develop, improve and widen the range of the Company's products.

His patient and painstaking investigation into better methods of manufacturing and in the setting of higher standards of quality laid a sound foundation on which the Company progressed and still influences its marketing to-day.

On relinquishing his production responsibilities he took over the organisation and control of the financial affairs of the Company and for over fifty years was its secretary until he became Chairman in 1958.

He was a quiet and reserved man but he took a keen interest in most aspects of the Company's affairs. His patience in listening to the views of others, his belief that the man on the job should always be consulted about the work in hand and any changes that were contemplated, was an inspiration to those who worked with him. He was always seeking better methods and encouraging others to help him in the search; his horizons were wide in all aspects.

In April, 1943, the same night that the Forest Gate factory was bombed, his own home was severely damaged, resulting in his going to Chesterfield, where he lived until his home was rebuilt after the war. During this time he made a great contribution in setting up the Company's organisation in Chesterfield, and made many friends in the district. His last visit to Chesterfield in 1958 was to present on behalf of the Company a silver loving cup to the collection of civic plate in the Town Hall.

Robertson dies: an affectionate obituary of Robert Robertson appeared in the November 1961 issue of The Trebor Magazine.

product. The firm was raising its game, and overseas was extending its reach. But Sydney Marks also had his mind on the leap of growth that comes through acquisition. By buying scores of small businesses in the decade after the war, he had gained share and raised output. Now, however, he wanted to acquire something a bit larger.

Preparing the sons for the business

JOHN MARKS

One of the chief ingredients of a family firm is, unsurprisingly, family, so Sydney Marks' two sons were raised from an early age to play their part in the business. Their older sister Diana was less involved with the firm; she trained as a teacher then studied art at St Martin's in London.

John first learnt to boil sugar during the school holidays when he was paid ten pence halfpenny per hour. After school at Oundle and national service in Germany, he went to Clare College Cambridge then joined the firm in 1953. He started at Forest Gate, working in various departments, before heading north to become works superintendent in Chesterfield. 1957 saw him move to the advertising agency Erwin

Wasey, Ruthrauff & Ryan, working on campaigns across other industries, before going to Maidstone in 1961 when the firm bought Sharps.

His brother Ian went to Rugby School, then spent two years with the Royal Engineers for his national service. He also went to Clare College, Cambridge, where he studied economics. Holidays were spent learning how to boil sugar at Forest Gate. On leaving Cambridge, he too joined the firm straightaway, heading off to Austria and Germany for six months immersion in sweet making. Then it was back to Forest Gate and up to Chesterfield for fifteen months as works superintendent.

IAN MARKS

Bill Deighan

Bill Deighan remembers

'When I joined the company in 1948, I was a production engineer working at Forest Gate. Ian was a young chappie and he and John would appear with Sydney in the workshop. They'd bring toys which they'd broken and I'd repair them. As they got older, the toys got bigger. Soon it was go-carts. While John and Ian were at university they spent their holiday breaks in the factory; they clocked in and they clocked out each day – and they worked on the slabs doing the heavy work. They would do the cooking, which was very hot, probably in the nineties even with the huge amount of air-conditioning and extraction. They had a good grounding in the hands-on part of it all.'

Sharps

Buying its rival Sharps Toffees made Trebor one of the largest sugar confectioners in the land.

The first Trebor Magazine of 1961 announced to staff: 'Hardly had we entered the New Year than we received the news that Trebor had acquired the old established firm of Edward Sharp & Sons, Ltd., the famous toffee makers, of Maidstone, Kent. We welcome them in the Trebor family and hope that as the years go by we shall enjoy beneficial co-operation with the family of Sir Kreemy Knut.' For £750,000 Trebor had bought another long-established family sweet firm, comprising a brand (Sharps Toffees), an icon (Sir Kreemy Knut), a business in trouble and a large but old-fashioned factory in Maidstone (whose workers had long been mad about their cricket team).

Sharps was of course a competitor, though toffees trailed far behind mints and boiled sweets in the Trebor catalogue. This acquisition gave the firm real weight in the toffee sector, plus significant chocolate production and a printing subsidiary to produce packaging which it renamed Printway. A new research and development department was set up at Maidstone, while some areas of the factory there were expanded and re-equipped. Rather than amalgamate the two businesses, Sydney Marks decided to keep Sharps as a separate concern within the Trebor Group and in 1964 appointed John Marks its managing director. It was only in 1968 that the businesses merged – along with Moffat and the overseas companies – to become Trebor Sharps Ltd.

Sir Kreemy Knut

A dapper young gent, memorably monocled with cane and bowler hat, Sir Kreemy Knut first appeared in 1919 as the face of Sharps Toffee. The word 'knut', meaning a dedicated follower of fashion, appeared around the time of the first world war, and was gloriously referenced in a 1914 music hall song by Arthur Wimperis: *'I'm Gilbert the Filbert, the knut with a K, the pride of Piccadilly, a blasé roué.'*

After the second world war, Sharps brought him back. As Nicholas Whittaker recounts in Sweet Talk: 'Sharps resurrected Sir Kreemy Knut, pressing him into service as a mascot for their toffee – as a live person. Not, alas, a dotty member of the aristocracy, but a rep named Nobby Clarke, co-opted from the

Sir Kreemy Knut reappeared on Sharps advertising throughout the 20th century.

sales force. Arriving by Rolls, Sir Kreemy was a regular visitor at shows and seaside resorts during the Fifties. A pocket hero at only 5ft, he was a great favourite with the children.' He also appeared as a marionette with the Sharps

Toffees Puppet Theatre. Forty years later in 1994 Monkhill Confectionery reintroduced the character to relaunch their Sharps of York range. Today Sir Kreemy Knut exists mostly as a highly collectible metal figurine.

Sharps was founded in 1876, when the twenty-two year old Mr Edward Sharp borrowed £50 off his father to open a grocery shop in Week Street, Maidstone. He went on to build a warehouse and stables behind the shop, but the wholesale business did not prosper. Meantime his wife Clara boiled up sweets from recipes passed down in her family. She put these into the shop and they did prosper, so Edward decided to concentrate on confectionery. He brought in a sugar boiler called Edmund Frost and started selling his goods around the Medway towns of Kent. They were an immediate hit, the firm grew strongly during the 1890s and by 1911 Sharp needed to build a large factory to meet demand. He started building in St Peter Street, Maidstone, beside the River Medway and the factory was popularly christened the 'Kreemy Works.' By 1921 Sharps had become world leader in toffee, helped by the distinctive Kreemy Nougat advertising. Edward Sharp was rewarded by being made baronet in 1922. In 1947 Sharps was granted a Royal Warrant, which became inherited by Trebor with the title 'By appointment to Her Majesty Queen Elizabeth II Confectioners.'

Below: nicknamed the Kreemy Works, the Sharps factory in Maidstone seen here in 1970 was one of the Kent town's main employers through much of the twentieth century. *Below left:* these boys sort batches of toffee during the 1920s. *Below right:* between the wars Sharps opened its own £10,000 sports ground.

BRILLIANT BATTING BY A. P. F. CHAPMAN & AMES

Opening of Kreemy Works Sports Ground at Maidsto. e.

One of the pleasantest places in Maidstone on Wednesday was Messrs. Edward Sharp and Sons' magnificent new £10,000 sports ground in London Road. Eighteen months ago this land was a cherry orchard and garden adjoining Mr. J. C. Hubble's house. Now it is one of the finest equipped sports grounds in the county and a monument to the generous interest the famous toffee firm displays in the after-factory welfare of its employees. There are bowls greens, hard and grass tennis courts, and a splendid sward, smooth as a billiard table, on which, on

Left: Sharps remained a separate brand until Trebor Sharps was formed in 1968. This cutting edge Commer van of 1963 – featuring a walk-through interior in which the driver could directly access stock – was decorated to support a special promotion of the 'my word' toffee assortment.

Sharps Easter Eggs

Back in 1935 Sharps became famous for creating giant Easter Eggs, each weighing 27.5lbs. Part of their appeal were the decorative flowers, handmade from marzipan by an expert team at the Maidstone factory. The chocolate eggs were made on a Jensen Hollow Goods Moulding Plant, bought from Denmark in 1954 and later extended into a 154ft long giant of temperature controlled production. Each year the eggs became

more striking, promoting the firm at a time when chocolate, rather than sugar, ruled the day. Rising chocolate prices made the monster eggs too uneconomic for production after 1964, but the 2.25lb 'Treasure Basket' egg, packed with fudge and toffees remained popular, not least with the royal family who gave Sharps, and the group, the distinction of a royal warrant. Company mythology recalls a thankyou letter from a lady-in-waiting who wrote, 'I was delighted to lay your egg before the princess.'

SHARPS STILL THE WORD FOR TOFFEE

The new alchemy of marketing

As sales techniques matured from shifting boxes to inciting demand, so Trebor explored fresh ways to make customers want its products.

With rationing a distant memory, the nation wealthier and consumers ever more picky, the 1960s spurred progress in the way goods were brought to market. New disciplines like marketing and merchandising took their place in business planning. Manufacturers started working more closely with wholesalers and retailers. Like any forward-thinking business, especially one embracing both manufacture and distribution, Trebor sought to stay ahead of this curve.

From 1960 onwards, the firm developed merchandising teams to support their salesforce. Rather than simply sell boxes of goods, these merchandisers worked with shops to ensure Trebor products were well displayed and promoted. They were helped by the arrival of new units and dispensers for displaying sweets at their point of sale. 1965 saw the arrival of a dedicated marketing department. Advertising was no longer ad-hoc; the firm now timed campaigns to support the launch of new products, and made greater use of research to ensure its ads reached the right targets.

The first Trebor TV commercial aired in 1958 for the launch of *Sonnets*; its initial campaign targeted Lancashire. Unfortunately the product bombed, so Sydney Marks sped up the launch of *Bitter-Orange* and *Bitter-Lemon*. Ads for these appeared in the Southern TV area. While *Bitter-Orange* sold poorly, *Bitter-Lemon* proved a hit; later sold in the US as Regal Crown *Sour Lemons*, this product proved crucial to the firm later winning a Queen's Award for Industry.

From then on, TV advertising became a regular component of Trebor promotion. The most successful ad in 1965 used ventriloquist Terry Hall and his dummy Lenny the Lion to promote *Trebor Extra Strong Mints*. Also in 1965 Sharps went to Paris to film a 90 second long 'Spectacular' TV spot – rare in length for those days – featuring a dancer, full orchestra and 'Britain's leading trumpeter Kenny Baker'. Other promotions took a more conventional route; the *Trebor Twins* and the *Glitter Girls* toured the nation, offering prizes to those who could prove they had a bag of Trebor product in their pockets.

Above left: TV advertisements heralded the arrival of Bitter-Orange and Bitter-Lemon at the end of the 1950s. Thanks to the new marketing budgets, it had become a lot more expensive to launch new products.

RIGHT: sales of Extra Strong Mints shot up when Lenny the Lion sold them on TV with the help of the voice and fingers of Terry Hall. Earlier the firm had tried using a real-live big cat, the Trebor Lion, shown in one ad being walked in the park by a young woman. But ventriloquism sold more.

BELOW: two young models named Maureen and Rosemary were sent around South Wales and the West Country in 1963 as the Trebor Twins. They had vans and costumes to promote Bitter-Lemon and Bitter-Orange. TV ads told customers to keep a packet handy at home in case the Twins came to call; then if they answered a question correctly, they would win a prize – maybe a giant teddy bear or even an electric clock. During the month-long promotion the Twins called on over two thousand houses. That's a lot of gates to open and dogs to avoid.

BELOW: Sharps made TV history in 1965 with a spot lasting 90 seconds. It featured a dancer parading beside the top four lines: Top Cream, Chocolate Top Cream, My Word and Assorted Super-Kreem.

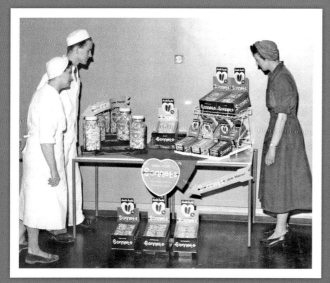

LEFT: Forest Gate employees get to see new packaging and point-of-display units for the Sonnets launch in 1958.

Hilda Clark retires

Miss Hilda Clark was one of the leading figures in the firm's history. A Forest Gate native who joined the chocolate department in 1918 while in her teens, she went on to build and manage the Chesterfield operations until retiring in 1963. Her leaving party was a grand event. As one attendee recalled, 'It was at the Savoy of course, the Marks family's favourite stamping ground, and was organised personally by Sydney Marks with champagne, a meal, music, dancing and all the rest. When the meal was finished we were all invited to go down to the riverside entrance … where, standing in his uniform and peak cap, was Jack the old Forest Gate driver. He had been a lorry driver but when he got to sixty, Jack couldn't go on humping things around, so he went over to Trebor House as chauffeur. He used to take old Mrs Robertson out every Friday to the hairdressers, but that night he was there, standing by a brand new car. Sydney said to Hilda, "Get into your car and Jack will take you for a drive around the block." It was her retirement present – altogether more lavish than what anyone else got.'

Below: Sydney puffs another of his hundred daily cigarettes while Hilda Clark speaks at one of her retirement parties.

But given what she'd achieved for the firm, she deserved it. At that crucial time in 1941 when the firm's war contracts were being threatened by its London location, and many experienced managers were away fighting, she led the move up to the safer location of Chesterfield, first to set up a distribution facility but then to build and run a manufacturing operation. When derationing arrived in 1954, she made sure Chesterfield was able to ramp up production overnight to meet the surge in demand; by then she personally oversaw more production than the entire firm had achieved just before the war. She gave her life to the company, living in Room 23 of the Station Hotel Chesterfield until she retired.

A US magazine reports on the UK

From Time Magazine, 22nd April 1962

Britons gobble more candy per capita (8oz weekly) than any other people in the world. As a result, they also have more toothaches than most – which has no apparent effect on candy consumption but causes a perpetual headache in the higher echelons of government, since the great majority of Britain's population gets its teeth fixed for nominal fees by the National Health Service. Though it collects taxes on every other luxury from dancing to death, the government has never levied a tax on sweets, as the British call their favorite vice.

Last week Chancellor of the Exchequer Selwyn Lloyd, a man never hitherto famed for political audacity, slapped a 15% tax on candy, ice cream and soda pop. Britons, shocked to their cavities by what many soon called "the Lollipop Budget," protested that it was a "tax on children," though craving for candy knows no age limits. The government will collect $140 million a year from the sweet-tooth tax – which makes it a classic bit of budget balancing, since the government now pays exactly $140 million yearly to dentists to repair the damage.

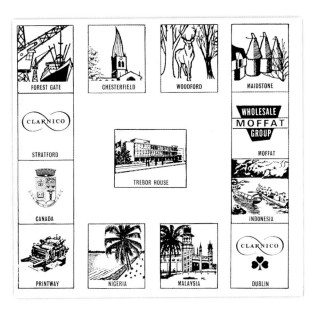

Below: Trebor Nigeria is born, as reported in The Trebor Magazine in Autumn 1962.

P.S.
On September 12, the following cables were exchanged.

From Christlieb, Lagos
" FORMALITIES COMPLETED TREBOR NIGERIA NOW IN EXIST-ENCE"

Mr. Sydney replied:
" TREBOR NIGERIA - CONGRATU-LATIONS MANY HAPPY RETURNS OF THE DAY"
POPPA TREBOR.

Working Together

The company magazine Working Together first appeared in July 1953. For many years it was edited by Mr AG Allan, who had served as a sergeant with Sydney Marks during the war before becoming transport manager at the Chesterfield factory. The cover of the company magazine *(above)* during the 1960s and 1970s often showed graphical representations of each geographical entity within the Trebor family group. The cranes for Forest Gate may refer to the nearby docks and Tate & Lyle sugar refinery at Silvertown. The crooked spire of Chesterfield was famous, as were the oast houses of Kent near Maidstone. Deer were not regular visitors to Woodford plant, though Epping Forest was nearby.

Left: the Trebor Magazine of July 1960 shows a rep giving a one pound premium bond prize to a similarly dapper shopkeeper.

Mr. Trebor Calls

" Have you a roll of TREBOR BITTER LEMON?"
" Ah! Thank you very much. And what's this? An Outer of Bitter Lemon and an Outer of Bitter Orange side by side on your counter! Mr. Retailer, I am very pleased to introduce myself as Mr. Trebor and to give you this voucher for a £1 Premium Bond which you have won because of your display." " Congratulations! and lots of good luck with the Premium Bond! "
The above conversation, or something like it, has taken place in well over a hundred shops in the Northern Television area this Spring. The object was to encourage retailers not only to stock these two lines which are being heavily advertised but to give them a really good display within reach of the customer.
If current sales figures are anything to go by, the scheme has certainly made its contribution to our success.
It was based on the efforts of Miss Trebor in London last year but this time the Northern Team of Canvassers took it in turn to play the role of " Lady Bountiful " under a masculine title. Our illustration shows Mr. D. E Howell, the Canvassing Supervisor, handing over the first voucher to be given out to Mr. Clarke of Liverpool.
Altogether Mr. Trebor will have made over a thousand calls in the North and Western area. If Bitter Lemon and Bitter Orange are not on display or in stock, he leaves

LG Pattison was Sydney Marks' adjutant during the war before joining the firm in 1956 to marshal the marketing of new products such as Sonnets and Bitter Lemons. In 1959 he became marketing director of Jameson's, a chocolate sweet maker with whom Trebor had strong links.

Commonwealth expansion

Trebor found it easier to export to countries within the British Commonwealth. Nigeria and West Africa were major markets for the firm.

A good way to appreciate the global nature of business today is to look back fifty years. Half a century ago, it was much tougher to export goods. Many countries were simply not open for business, their indigenous industries protected by walls of tariffs. It was hard to communicate with foreign offices: calling them was expensive and unreliable, you could send some words by telex or telegram, but most papers had to take the post. Given these barriers, it's little surprise that British businesses often traded best in Commonwealth countries where, thanks to the imperial history, there were easier commercial links.

Nigeria

A good example is Nigeria. Trebor first sent sweets out to this West African country in the 1940s and by the 1960s it sold more mints there than in any other overseas market. At one time sales of *Trebor Mints* in Nigeria exceeded those in Britain. Compressed sweets suited the hot climate and had a good shelf life. It was claimed that you could stand in any village in Nigeria and shout 'Trebor' and everyone would come running. During the Nigerian civil war of the late 1960s, *Trebor Mints* were said to be used as currency. Together with Ghana, Uganda, Rhodesia (now Zimbabwe), Tanganyika (now Tanzania) and Egypt, West Africa was by far the largest sales area in the world for Trebor.

Freddie Farman *became export sales manager in 1956 and spent years building Trebor's connections with customers abroad.*

Right: *as with Trebor's factories in Britain, the majority of employees in Nigeria were women.*

The firm's partner in Nigeria – the Christlieb family – was identified by Sydney H Marks back in the 1930s. His son Sydney strengthened the relationship by founding Trebor Nigeria with them in 1961. Two years later they started building a factory at Apapa near Lagos. This was revolutionary – a British company not simply harvesting the resources of an ex-colony, but creating its own manufacturing business there. Yet making the sweets locally brought risks back home: it sharply cut production in the firm's UK factories which, until then, had been supplying the overseas market.

Sidney Bonner, the company engineer who had led the creation of works at Chesterfield and Woodford, was sent out to oversee the building of the new factory. As one contemporary recalls, 'We shipped out several refurbished old presses and roll-wrapping machines which had been superceded in England and a British works manager trained in compressing. Sugar had to be imported because local sugar was not of the quality required; we installed generators because the local electricity supply was so uncertain and we dug bore holes to ensure sufficient water supply.' The factory soon became a local landmark; ships entering Lagos harbour at night would use the light on its roof as a navigational aid.

John Christlieb was the chief executive of Trebor Nigeria, a larger than life character who knew how to operate in the country. A trained pilot, he was said to buy planes locally, then fly them to England for sale and unofficial currency transfer. But Trebor Nigeria never repeated the success of the 1960s. Civil war and political uncertainty made it difficult to trade, let alone take revenues out of the country; moreover the government demanded a steady dilution of foreign ownership of local industries. By the late 1970s Trebor had become a minority holder in the company it had established.

Above: *John Marks entertains some 'Mammy Traders' – the businesswomen so crucial to distributing Trebor products in Nigeria.*

Above: *in the 1960s Nigeria accounted for more than half the total population across West Africa. Mints sold particularly well in the muslim north, where little alcohol was consumed and peppermint was a popular relief for dry throats caused by dust storms from the Sahara.*

Southeast Asia

From the former colonies of Malaysia and Hong Kong, Trebor advanced across Asia.

Malaysia

Another former British colony to discover the joys of Trebor sweets was Malaysia, known as the Malaysian Federation when Sydney Marks announced his plans in 1964. His chosen partner was Boustead, a long-established business with interests in many different industries. Together they planned to set up a factory in Petaling Jaya, near Kuala Lumpur. As usual, engineering expert Sidney Bonner was sent out to find a location, organise construction and equip the factory; this time he needed to convert a derelict tile-making works, so his experience at converting the factories in Chesterfield and Woodford came in useful. Plant and machinery were sent out from England and Germany, while local labour carried out building and installation. The factory was considered the most up to date confectionery house in the Far East, creating most types of Trebor product including high boilings, chocolate-centred sweets, toffees, chews and compressed mints.

Above: elegant cinema usherettes prepare to sell Trebor goods to Kuala Lumpur moviegoers in 1960.

To manage the factory, the firm found Ray Hardless, who had served with the British army and brought good local knowledge. Few of the new employees had any experience of producing sweets. As the company magazine reported, 'There were many laughs at the expense of the moulding girls, who at first hung on to the sugar too long, thus losing their gloves in a sticky mess. From this experience they soon learned their lesson, however, and in two or three days were quite adept.' Indeed the first shipment of sweets set off for Penang within three weeks of the factory starting operations. Later on the firm appointed Alan Bailey from soon-to-be acquired Clarnico as managing director in Malaysia.

Right: a Trebor delivery van in Thailand.

Sidney Bonner in action

Late in the afternoon of 25th November 1964 the group engineer Sidney Bonner arrived in Kuala Lumpur. Within half an hour he was visiting potential sites for a Trebor factory. One was promising. He spent two and a half days negotiating its purchase, then headed off for a few days in Australia to meet up with Trebor colleagues. Three days later he returned to conclude the purchase in Kuala Lumpur. Then he flew onto Lagos to start up plant for high boilings for Trebor Nigeria. With this achieved, he headed back to London. Without the ingenuity and energy of managers such as Bonner, the firm would never have expanded so well overseas.

Lagos 1962: Sidney Bonner digs the first hole to start construction of Trebor's factory in Nigeria.

Indonesia

In 1970 the firm's Malaysian partner Boustead persuaded Sydney Marks to consider operations in Indonesia. This vast country – 17,500 islands strung along an archipelago as wide as the United States – was home to many millions of sweet-lovers, while economic conditions had stabilised since Suharto had taken power from Sukarno in 1967. But in 1970 the government did not allow foreigners to invest in confectionery. So Trebor set up a venture with a Chinese Indonesian partner to build a glucose factory, which *was* permitted. As local MD Terry Spurling recalled, 'We got a licence for going in there with our knowledge of glucose. Not that Trebor had ever run a glucose plant before, we just got it from our supplier like sugar. Confectionery was allowed by the licence because we persuaded them that sweets were a downstream by-product of glucose making. So we were the first foreign confectionery company to operate in Indonesia.'

Sidney Bonner helped again in equipping the factory, but this time he also needed to find machines to produce glucose from tapioca starch, a root widely available in Indonesia. This was also a new activity for the firm, but soon glucose became a major business in itself, drawing customers from throughout the main Indonesian island of Java and providing half of the operation's turnover. Later on, the Chesterfield works engineer John Hall went out to help manage the factory.

John Marks made regular visits to the country and remembered a golf competition in which President Suharto was taking part. 'Suharto was the winner,' he noted, 'but curiously his name had been engraved on the cup even before the contest took place.'

Above right, Hong Kong: from 1953 the firm's sales in the colony were managed by Fonson & Co. In 1970 the Robertson Wilson trading company took over, importing Trebor products on some of the first large containers to reach Hong Kong. By 1981 the colony had become a territory and the John D Hutchison company handled distribution of products, such as those featured here.

Inflation problems in Jakarta

Terry Spurling went out to Indonesia in 1978 to head up the operation. 'Here I was, thirty three years old, managing director, with two small kids, and I'm the only ex-pat in the company.' Two hundred people then worked for Trebor Indonesia, across the factory and in sales teams. Sales were strong but the market was very price sensitive. It also suffered from serious inflation – a particular problem with sweets sold by weight rather than in count lines. 'At first most sweets were sold to people with small stalls, the price being five rupiah a piece. But inflation ran at about 20% a year. Seven years later we still sold them at five rupiah each, but we'd had to make the sweets smaller to counter the inflation. We couldn't do this any more, so decided to raise the prices by 25% while making the product larger.' Unfortunately this co-incided with a government decision to devalue the currency by half. 'So volume dropped because no-one's got any money and we'd just decided to raise prices to cover past inflation. The government now started accusing capitalists of undermining the local economy by profiteering, so we were under pressure to drop the price back to five rupees, which would have killed us as material costs had gone up so much.' Fortunately Spurling was able to overcome this problem and Indonesia continued to be an important market for the firm in Southeast Asia.

Production in Jakarta started in January 1971.

A global name

During the 1960s Trebor sold well around the world. North America, Europe, Asia and Australasia all performed strongly. Thanks to this export success, the firm won one of the first Queen's Awards for Industry.

The toast is Trebor: *Field Marshal Earl Alexander of Tunis and Sydney John stand before the insignia for the Queen's Award to Industry at the 1966 ceremony in Trebor House.*

In 1966 The Queen's Award to Industry (now known as the Queen's Award for Enterprise) was set up to recognise British companies which performed particularly strongly. Trebor was among the first food companies to be so honoured, and the only one within the confectionery industry. In July 1966 Field Marshal Earl Alexander of Tunis came along to the Trebor House canteen to give Sydney John the award in front of 200 guests and employees.

Trebor won the award for 'outstanding and sustained export achievement', particularly for the firm's recent success in America. Ian Marks remembered Chesterfield factory creaking under the pressure of making over a hundred tons a week of Regal Crown *Sour Lemons* for the US; more than 3000 tons of this popular candy were exported there altogether. Freddie Farman and his international sales team were central to this success. As *The Times* reported on 5th May 1966, 'Robertson & Woodcock has more than doubled its overseas trade in the past four years and now sells to some 50 countries. More than 20% of output from three factories in the UK is exported, over half to dollar markets.'

These baggage handlers look surprisingly smart while publicising the air freight of Sharps product to Germany.

Above: never an easy country to export to, Japan took some time to deliver profits for Trebor. Good local managers helped create a small, steady business for the firm there.

Above: thanks to Thorvald Pedersen, Denmark became the firm's first export market in 1930. Here is a 1969 Trebor Pick-n-Mix display in the Anva department store in Copenhagen.

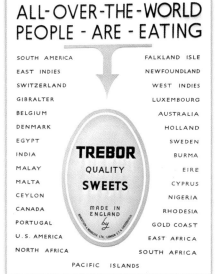

ALL-OVER-THE-WORLD PEOPLE - ARE - EATING

SOUTH AMERICA	FALKLAND ISLE
EAST INDIES	NEWFOUNDLAND
SWITZERLAND	WEST INDIES
GIBRALTER	LUXEMBOURG
BELGIUM	AUSTRALIA
DENMARK	HOLLAND
EGYPT	SWEDEN
INDIA	BURMA
MALAY	EIRE
MALTA	CYPRUS
CEYLON	NIGERIA
CANADA	RHODESIA
PORTUGAL	GOLD COAST
U.S. AMERICA	EAST AFRICA
NORTH AFRICA	SOUTH AFRICA

TREBOR QUALITY SWEETS MADE IN ENGLAND *by*

PACIFIC ISLANDS

Left: some top Finnish salesmen visit Trebor Head Office in the early 1980s.

Left: Alan Scott, assistant export sales manager, proudly holds up the first box inscribed with the new export award.

Below: remarkable sales of Regal Crown Sours for the US market helped win Trebor's Queen's Award to Industry.

Above right: New Jersey-based Tootsie Roll Candies trumpeted the 1966 arrival in New York of two 20' containers holding 65,000 lbs of Trebor 10 cent rolls: the first sweets to arrive in this way and the first Trebor goods to be distributed by Tootsie. Sadly, Tootsie failed to capitalise on Trebor's huge prior success in North America. In time the firm turned instead to sales agents, over whom it gradually increased control.

Left: in 1963, having long relied on Germany for new technology and production methods, the firm decided to return the compliment and sell its own products there. Glitter Fruits and Glitter Mints were chosen to spearhead the venture, with Bitter Cherry soon a popular addition. Such high quality lines were more likely to succeed than cheap sweets which faced competition from subsidised factories beyond the Iron Curtain. Clive Robertson headed over to help LG Pattison set up the office in Hamburg. They recruited ten salesmen, created a German TV ad and so established the Trebor's first foothold within the Common Market. Here is the sales team in 1965 with their cars.

Clarnico

Another old East End sweet firm joined the group in 1969. Clarnico, famous for its *Mint Creams*, brought new lines and increased market share.

By the late 1960s Trebor Sharps had successfully integrated its two named firms and their product ranges, but was still hungry for acquisition. This time the directors did not have to look far. Clarnico was an East End manufacturer of peppermint creams and other sweets, with a main factory in Hackney Wick and a longer history than Robertson & Woodcock. Buying the business gave Trebor Sharps a wider product range and more manufacturing muscle. It also enabled the group to call itself 'the leader' in British sweets: aside from the chocolate giants Mars, Cadbury and Rowntree, Trebor Sharps was now the leader in sugar-based sweets, ahead of competitors such as Bassett and Barker & Dobson. Clarnico chairman George Mathieson left to run the property interests which Trebor chose not to buy while chief executive Bob Morrison took over a christmas cracker operation which the firm also declined to take on.

The purchase took place in 1969. Rather than keep the new business separate, as with Sharps, Sydney Marks swiftly combined the two businesses, subsuming sales and overhead functions within 70 days. Fearing competition to the Trebor brand, he cut the Clarnico product range to its best selling lines, ignoring advice that such competition was fine, so long as he controlled it. He also decided quickly to transfer production from the old, uneconomic factory to the group's plant at Maidstone; this was achieved by 1972. There were problems with the ancient machinery from Hackney, which one executive described as 'stuck together with sugar' and which proved difficult to work in Maidstone. There were also to be financial problems from a Clarnico subsidiary in Ireland. These, plus the cost of financing the acquisition, meant the group paid dearly during the early 1970s for its new market share.

New product ranges

Clarnico was best known for its *Mint Creams*, mint flavoured fondant creams which were crystallised to keep the cream soft. Together with *Chocolate Mint Creams*, which cased the creams in fine dessert chocolate, Clarnico dominated this sector of the market. Its jellies came in two forms: *Fruit Jellies* made with real fruit and *Sunshine Jellies* made with artificial flavours. Its *Pancho* range of panned chocolate sweets were made by adding chocolate in separate measured amounts to centres being rotated in a copper pan; these came in both peanut and raisin versions. *Dairy Fudge* was another market-leader for Clarnico; while fudge was new to Trebor, its manufacture was similar in process to toffee and caramel, which the firm had long produced. Other best sellers at this time for Clarnico were *Rum Truffles*, *Mitcham Mints* (more medicinal than *Trebor Mints*) and the *Good Evening Chocolates* and *Candies* assortments.

Charles Woodhouse remembers

'The Clarnico deal was very exciting. It helped me cut my teeth as a young lawyer. Everything came to a head during an all-night completion meeting, a common event today but rare back then. They were trying to drag things out with new questions about the Stratford property. In the end Ian Marks said, "I've got a banker's draft in my pocket to buy this business for cash. Either we have a deal tonight or I walk away." Given this was a £900,000 deal, that was a bold statement – but it worked. We got the company.'

1952 Clarnico advertisement.

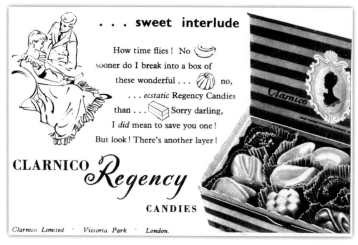

. . . sweet interlude

How time flies! No
sooner do I break into a box of
these wonderful . . . no,
. . . ecstatic Regency Candies
than . . . Sorry darling,
I *did* mean to save you one!
But look! There's another layer!

CLARNICO *Regency*
CANDIES

Clarnico Limited · Victoria Park · London.

A grand old firm, down on its luck

Clarnico was the trading name for Clarke, Nickolls & Coombs, a firm established in 1872 by George Gray and George Barrow to produce candied peel. They started operations in Hackney Wick, a short distance across East London from Trebor's original base in Forest Gate, soon moving into marmalade, jam and then confectionery. By 1895 their trade price list included such gems as *Chinese Pigtails* and *Hangman's Noose* (both liquorice), *Toasted Haddocks* and *Mutton Chops* (based on coconut), *Pig's Head & Carrots, Dolly's Musical Bottles* and *Ching Chang Watches*. Later on they became known for fudge, iced caramels, fruit jellies and – most famously – peppermint creams.

The firm's location in Hackney Wick was right beside the River Lee navigation canal, enabling easy delivery of sugar and coal for the furnaces; this also saved money, for ships in the Thames could offload directly onto barges which went up the Lee, so avoiding the high charges of the London Authorities Docks. German bombers destroyed much of the Clarnico works in October 1940. After four years of negotiation with the War Damage Commission, the owners decided to rebuild on the spot and finished their new factory in 1952. Unfortunately they got their timing wrong, building a traditional multi-storey factory on a relatively small footprint. Within a few years the fork lift truck would revolutionise the layout of industrial works, enabling long production lines to be laid out on vast single floors. Moreover, the lack of building materials after the war meant the factory was poorly constructed. It was not a difficult decision for Trebor Sharps in 1969 to shift Clarnico production out to its own works.

A PETITION lies here for Signature on behalf of GEORGE NEWTON who was sentenced to death at the Central Criminal Court last Friday, 13th inst. for the Wilful Murder of Ada Roker on Xmas eve. NEWTON was at one time employed in the Wood Box Dept., and left about a year ago. Any worker wishing to sign the petition can do so in the Gatekeeper's Lodge, or in the Dining Hall.

Clarnico was a huge East London sweet firm even before Robertson & Woodcock was founded. The **top** picture from 1908 shows the employees leaving work; there must be at least a thousand of them here. The company was very proud of its private fire brigade (**above**, also 1908) which served both the factory and the surrounding area of Stratford. **Left** is an oddity from the Clarnico archive – a petition on behalf of an ex-employee who had been sentenced to death.

Clarnico's new factory at Hackney Wick in East London was completed in 1951 but out-of-date by the time Trebor bought the company in 1969. Its location is now within the site of the London 2012 Olympic Games; to be precise, beneath the International Press Centre, in an area to be named Sweetwater after the games.

A social business

The company magazine loved to feature Christmas celebrations, dinner dances, theatre trips and kids' parties from around the country.

RIGHT: service with a smile as Chesterfield celebrates Christmas 1955 in the works canteen.

ABOVE: Saturday 22nd February 1958 saw the first outing of the 'Trebor Drivers' Social Club' in London's glittering West End. First stop was The Chicken Inn, Leicester Square (pictured), then on to the Palace Theatre to see Norman Wisdom in 'Where's Charley?'.

RIGHT: they knew how to party back in the 1970s. Here are some Forest Gate employees enjoying a Social in May 1972 at the Little Bardfield County Club in Essex.

BELOW: John Marks displays his skills with a hula hoop at a Chesterfield dinner dance in 1959.

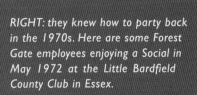

ABOVE: 6th December 1958. Time for a Christmas party for the directors and senior executives at the Cafe Royal in London.

Once again the Clarnico sports and social club held their fourth "Cockney Night" event in the main dining hall on May 2nd. It was well supported with a crowd of some 368 folks. Many of these included our colleagues from Forest Gate and Woodford. The running buffet which consisted of "Fish and Chips" and "Saveloys and Pease Pudding" was very popular. "Cockney Night" is something with a difference. The arrangements were made by Jack Musgrave. As can obviously be seen the evening went with a swing.

All proceeds will go to the pensioners party fund.

ABOVE: the Clarnico 'Cockney Night' in May 1970.

ABOVE: it's a Friday night dinner dance for the firm in January 1973. Every lady receives a rose, there's dancing to the Del Gray Quartet — and John Marks makes probably the shortest speech of his career when he simply proposes 'The Company'.

ABOVE: high jinks at the 1962 Annual Party.
BELOW: spring 1970 in South Wales.

ABOVE: during a 1960 factory outing to see the Blackpool Illuminations, these Chesterfield employees take a few moments out for some refreshments.

BELOW: on 4th January 1958, eighty children sat down to a Christmas party in the Forest Gate canteen. Aged five to eight, they enjoyed games, sweets and a film show. Two weeks later, 280 older children went to see Bertram Mills' Circus at Olympia, courtesy of the factory's Social Committee.

Christmas Party at Newport

The Gwent Confectionery Co., decided to be somewhat sophisticated this year and organised a dinner dance for staff and friends at the Westgate Hotel, Newport. The arrangements were made by Mrs. Strickland and, as can obviously be seen, the event was a great success.

Moffat

Trebor bought up tens of local distributors to create
Moffat – a national wholesaling group.

John Burnett Collins, known to most as J.B., was born in 1915 and worked as a stockbroker prior to the Second World War, where he served under colonel Denis Hedley, son-in-law of Robert Robertson and sales director of Robertson & Woodcock. After the war, knowing J.B. was unhappy to return to the stock market, Hedley invited him to meet Sydney Marks. As he later recalled, 'Sydney told me that Alec T Moffat, who had run an old-established boiled sweets and toffee business in Ardwick Green, a suburb of Manchester, had died and the business was up for sale. Would I like to take it over?'

Unsure about the offer as he knew nothing about confectionery, J.B. went to Manchester to take a look. On arrival he found some local lads booting a ball against the factory wall, and when he told them tersely to 'Hop it' one small boy equally tersely told him to 'xxxx off.' This cheeky response both amused and intrigued him, for he realised he would be back once again with the kind of men he knew well from the army, but this time he would be building his own business. So, with the firm's backing, he took over the company in 1950 and set about building Moffat into one of the country's major confectionery wholesalers.

Moffat was also known as the M Group – blessed with this faintly sinister logo, more redolent of a spy network than a wholesale chain.

A secret acquisition

This takeover was central to Sydney Marks' post-war acquisition plans. Moffat brought manufacturing plant, which was useful, but more importantly it gave the firm access to an established wholesale operation across the North West. Marks also put J.B. in charge of the newly acquired Bristol Sweet Supply Co and R&J Scholes Ltd. This grouping was known internally as The M Group but to the world it was Moffat – and together it offered a broad reach for wholesale. Yet outside the board of Trebor, J.B. and a few of his managers, the firm's ownership of Moffat was a secret.

At that stage, Marks did not feel Trebor could reveal it had a captive wholesaler. Traditionally wholesalers were independent, stocking products from competing manufacturers – as did Moffat – and people would assume (albeit correctly) that Trebor products got preference over their rivals in what should have been a level playing field. But while Trebor's own sales teams covered many territories, they could never achieve the depth of a wholesaler stocking not only confectionery but also tobacco and other products. So Trebor's sales figures benefitted hugely from Moffat's sales – and the link remained secret.

J.B. Collins *was persuaded by Sydney John to take over Moffat in 1950. He went on to turn it into one of the country's major confectionery wholesalers.*

Moffat merges with Trebor Sharps

In 1959 the firm made the connection public and Moffat continued to expand. J.B. was adept at acquiring small wholesalers on the brink of retirement – more than forty overall – and by 1965 Moffat operated 30 depots across the country. In 1971 the operation was merged with Trebor Sharps though it retained Moffat as a trading name. By that stage Trebor's percentage share of Moffat's throughput was significantly more than its 4-5% of the UK confectionery market. But Moffat took care to play fair and there were few complaints. In any case, Trebor products represented a small percentage of the Moffat catalogue, especially given the predominance of tobacco.

Revenues from wholesaling grew to become much greater than those from manufacturing, but the tiny margins meant that Moffat provided the group with far less profit than Trebor Sharps. Moreover the volume of stock required, especially at peak times like Christmas, meant Moffat was hungry for working capital, always at a premium in a private company. On the other hand, with inflation often in double figures during the 1970s, sitting on stock could be a profitable business – and it was always a good idea to fill the warehouses with cigarettes just before a Government Budget which might raise excise duties. Overall, Moffat's wholesale operations raised very different financial challenges to the sweet business, but group finance coped and the advantages of ownership were considerable.

Old names come together

Until 1971 Moffat was a collection of local wholesalers, most of whom kept their trading names. Some had longer history than the firm itself: George Gardiner of Ipswich was founded in 1883, while J Tolhurst of Polegate in Sussex dated back to 1867. When Moffat merged with Trebor Sharps in 1971, the network's sixteen branches were all rebranded Moffat, though old local loyalty continued to fuel rivalry for national sales contests.

Left: Heard's of Neath, R Baker & Sons of West Hartlepool and Warwick Confectionery were typical of the small wholesalers who became part of Moffat.

1969 saw the arrival at Moffat of Ted Gillespie, previously UK chief executive of the Spar group, who created for the firm a voluntary group of retailers called Superchoice. These shops relied largely, but not exclusively, on Moffat for stock, so enjoying good rates and providing the firm with reasonably secure outlets. As the 1970s progressed, Moffat joined the top three UK confectionery wholesalers and was the only one with truly national coverage.

Gradually Moffat's business changed as smaller CTNs (confectioners, tobacconists and newsagents) and off licenses became replaced by chain stores. But its focus on sales remained strong: most editions of the company magazine through the 1970s and 1980s hailed the success of top Moffat sales teams and there was always detailed coverage of the annual Superchoice members' conference in Majorca, Benidorm or some other Spanish resort.

J.B. retired in 1980, enjoying the firm's traditional Savoy send-off for top managers. His gifts included a clock radio, binoculars and a drinks cabinet on wheels, stocked with his favourite tipples. He was toasted by Moffat's then chief executive Jack Thompson, who said that the operation's turnover under J.B.'s steer had grown from £34,000 in 1950 to nearly £100 million. This wholesale empire, once so secret, remained a crucial part of Trebor's success through the 1980s.

Above: Ted Gillespie joined Moffat from the Spar supermarket chain. He went on to follow Malcolm Macarthur as group sales & marketing director in the 1980s.

Above right: when June Woolley won Trebor's Retailer of the Year competition in 1969, the prize was not just a set of steak knives and peer recognition – she won a whole new shop worth £6,000. At a special ceremony at Chesterfield, before much press attention, Sydney Marks presented her with the deeds to the new premises at Creswell near Worksop. She had originally come to the notice of Frost of Mansfield, her local Moffat distributor. Here she and her husband stand proudly before her prize.

Moffat-branded products

The Moffat Maid brand included products as varied as soft drinks and tights. Later on Moffat's logo appeared in the same fluttering flag design as all group companies.

Left: Moffat shows off its Superchoice concept at a trade show. By linking with the wholesaler, shops could receive preferential treatment.

Trebor pioneers non-returnable jars

At the end of the 1960s manufacturers still supplied sweets in glass jars. Wholesalers' warehouses were full of empty jars, each destined for return to the factory and a two shilling deposit. Trebor was the first sweet-maker to stop this practice, supplying disposable plastic jars made at Chesterfield on special German machinery. This expense was far preferable to the cost of returning and cleaning heavy glass ones.

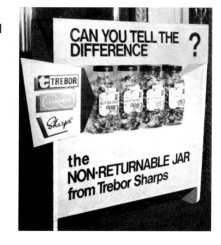

Reginald Woolsey: Frost & Co. Ltd. (Mansfield)— Aged 34 years and married. Has a son John aged 13 years and a daughter Linda aged 10 years.

I have faith in the Trebor goods I sell, but I think that persevering with my Trebor sample case has put me on the top in Trebor sales.

R. Woolsey
Frost & Co. Ltd.

Above: in August 1963 The Trebor Magazine asked top Moffat salesman Reg Woolsey why he thought he did well. Although he sold Trebor sweets, he saw himself as part of Frost & Co of Mansfield.

Left: successful Moffat salespeople and partners head off to Benidorm in Spain for a celebratory weekend in early 1973.

1970–1979

THE SEVENTIES

A new generation takes over. It invests ambitiously, explores new ways of working and keeps Trebor at the forefront of British sweetmaking.

All change

As the Sixties ended, many of the old certainties left with them. Soon Britain had to embrace a new currency and a new place within Europe. As customers and staff demanded more – and supermarkets found their muscles – firms like Trebor had to rethink how they did business.

The spring 1972 editorial from *Working Together* magazine gives a snapshot of how the group fared in the early 1970s. After several tough years, not helped by increases in purchase tax, 1971 saw increased sales, profits and market share in the UK. Both profit share and pensions were set to rise, Clarnico was now integrated, while Moffat was profiting from its national reorganisation. Overseas, sales were up but profitability was down. This was partly due to a spate of new factory openings: two plants now ran in Ireland, a new factory was being built in Nigeria, fresh facilities had just been completed in Indonesia and Canada and the factory in Malaysia was being extended. The magazine then reported that during the first six weeks of the year, Trebor sales staff had visited Switzerland, Austria, Italy, Canary Isles, Liberia, Ivory Coast, Spain, Germany, Nigeria and France. But dark clouds loomed on the economic horizon – higher costs, growing competition from overseas, rising inflation and political unrest both at home and abroad. Plus there were some structural changes to assimilate. In 1971 Britain had ditched the shilling and embraced the new decimal currency. In 1973 it was to join the EEC and open itself to Common Market legislation.

Confectionery faced challenges of its own. The price of sugar was rising. Retail price maintenance had been withdrawn several years before, so freeing prices and opening up a new era of discounting goods. With their prices no longer protected, independent sweet shops were disappearing in their hundreds. Grocery stores were introducing self-serve sweet counters. Traditional weigh-outs from jars gave way to countlines,

Above and right: anyone growing up in 1970s Britain can probably remember the pineapple and raspberry sweetness of Fruit Salad. Black Jacks were more of an acquired taste, with their aniseed kick and their habit of blackening your tongue. In 2003 the firm's new owners Cadbury declared that both lines were now out of favour with the public – so the Chesterfield factory, where they were then produced, was closed. Today both products are available through the Barratt brand, bought from Cadbury by Tangerine Confectionery.

attractively packaged for impulse buy. Most ominously, large retailers had been to America to see how low cost retailing – through supermarkets, convenience stores and out-of-town shopping centres – could shift power from manufacturers to retail chains. Now those large shops were poised with their merchandising plans and negotiating tactics to take on firms like Trebor.

Independent sweet shops were disappearing in their hundreds.

In response, Trebor reduced its number of lines to contain production costs. But it put more effort into the branding of its products, particularly the mints. In a more marketing-oriented world, where competitors used sophisticated tools to make consumers choose, and keep choosing, their products, such branding was crucial. The group invested more in marketing, trade and consumer promotions, and retraining the sales force for this new world. Forging more direct relations with customers, through brand loyalty, seemed like the best way for manufacturers like Trebor to gain greater bargaining power with the retail chains.

The true story of the policeman showered with glucose

One of the firm's most famous anecdotes is told by Bill Deighan, system works engineer at Forest Gate.

'We had this wonderful man called Oggy Avey working at Forest Gate. He'd been horribly injured in the desert fighting during the Second World War and he did various things at the factory such as manning the telephone exchange, receiving goods as doorkeeper. One day I was passing his little office and he calls me back. The look on his face told me something was up. He said Bill, I'm getting a bit concerned because the lollipop lady hasn't turned up. We had Shaftesbury Road School next door and a lot of the kids used to go home for lunch. This meant going across a very busy crossing between Shaftesbury Road and Katherine Road. What's more, we had lots of vehicles going over the forecourt delivering suppliers and one thing and another. Anyway, he said, I'm a bit worried because the lady hasn't turned up What are we going to do about it? So I'm thinking, I'll have to volunteer one of the engineers or something and I'm also thinking about the legality of providing somebody who's not trained. When lo and behold, up the road on his bicycle comes the cavalry in the shape of a local bobby who cycles over to us.
   Now a few minutes beforehand, a glucose tanker had pulled onto the forecourt and was connecting a pipe to our delivery point. We'd just walked away from the bobby when suddenly there's this horrendous explosion. We turned round and there's the policeman standing with at least a ton of hot sticky glucose dripping off him. It's running down his face and he's closed every orifice in his head, his eyes, his ears. His helmet's gone and his uniform is ruined. The road is two inches deep in glucose. Now, as you are probably aware, glucose has to be delivered warm, but once it hits a cold surface, it hardens. Meanwhile, as usual, somebody came to the rescue. And this somebody rushed over to the copper, who was trying to get this hardening glucose off his face. They grabbed him by the arm and took him into the lift up to the shower room. Somebody had to phone the local police station and tell them, we've got one of your policemen in our showers!

Oggy Avey in 1978

Early 70s

Integrating Clarnico – and paying for its acquisition – were big challenges at the start of the seventies.

In 1971 the group shifted production of Clarnico lines – fudge, jellies and creams – from Hackney Wick to Maidstone. This entailed a fair degree of re-organisation, especially moving the ancient machinery (still 'stuck together with sugar') and trying to make it work in the new location. Trebor opened the UK's largest confectionery distribution depot at Thamesmead in Kent and another depot in Birmingham to serve the Midlands. A new concept was launched which took off rapidly – mobile cash and carry vans to carry goods direct to retailers; the first unit was formed at the Hoddesdon depot with vans operating out of Plymouth, Birmingham and Manchester.

For many years retail grocers had united into voluntary groups to increase their buying power and so keep competitive with the chain stores. Moffat had launched Superchoice, the first voluntary group in the country for retail confectioners; each year the group took members on a jolly to Majorca.

Overseas the group took over the Leeds Candy Corporation in Montreal, acquired a minority holding in the West German distributor Markus and Walsh and formed a new company from the struggling Clarnico-Murray business in Dublin.

Financially, the group faced difficult times in 1972 and 1973. Debts from the Clarnico acquisition, coupled with the costs of new factories around the world, saw group borrowings reach record heights, while profits slipped in each of these

The master builder retires

In 1974 at the Savoy Hotel, Trebor bade farewell to the man responsible for building over 90% of the premises then used by employees worldwide. Sidney Bonner first met Sydney Marks when he came to install a new steam plant at Forest Gate in the mid 1930s. Marks invited him to join the firm in 1937 to organise the final extension of the Forest Gate factory. As chief engineer Bonner went on to organise the creation of Chesterfield factory during the war. After the war he built a plant at Lane Cove outside Sydney in Australia, then the two Nigerian factories in 1963 and 1970, the Malaysia facility in 1965 and the glucose and confectionery factory in Indonesia in 1970. Back in Britain he created Trebor House and the Woodford factory from the site of a coachbuilding works – and he went on to build all the Moffat depots. Like all great engineers, he was ingenious and capable. Trebor owes him much.

Sidney Bonner pictured in 1954.

years. But 1974 saw a turnaround and by 1975 the company was posting pre-tax profits of £3.2 million on turnover of £66.6 million.

Other developments

Not every new product succeeds – and the 1970s saw the failure of several high profile Trebor launches. *Buttersnap* was unable to make its mark in the chocolate snack market, while the *Swisskit* muesli-type bar proved too far ahead of its time. (Nowadays such cereal bars can be found on any confectionery counter). On the other hand the group did well with *Treborland*, a 'wonderful world' of comic characters designed to bolster the sagging market for *Chews* and other children's lines. The firm sometimes rode cannily on the coattails of famous characters. 'The Incredible Hulk' was a popular TV programme; Trebor's *Hunk Chew* bore a striking resemblance, or at least the word *Hunk* did.

This was a time when mass national promotions became standard for new products. A 'Globetrotter' competition, for example, distributed over four million leaflets and received 100,000 entries. Other major new product launches during the period were *Blobs* and *Double Agents*.

More than 300 salespeople worked for Moffat and Trebor Sharps' distribution arm, serving over 200,000 outlets across the UK. This distribution strength helped the group win the rights to sell US-firm Topps bubblegum in the UK, particularly its *Bazooka* brand. Moffat also used its national reach to support other, non-Trebor promotions: in 1978 it held the dubious distinction of helping the cartoon characters *The Smurfs* to promote National Benzole petrol stations. Today few have heard of National Benzole but many, sadly, can still recall *The Smurfs*.

Behind the scenes Jack Weekes was busy developing the research and development team at Maidstone, alongside Peter Antonelli's technical team, to build a more scientific approach to developing new products. This period also saw the birth of mass computerisation. Head office had bought its first computer in 1966, a huge IBM model, which it used for management accounts and producing invoices; now the group installed a mini-computer in each depot to speed up the processing of orders.

The muesli bar Swisskit was too far ahead of its time.

New Thamesmead depot

Above: *the floor for the cool house being laid at Trebor's new confectionery distribution depot at Thamesmead in Kent — the country's largest such facility when built in 1973.*

In 1973 the group built a massive new depot at Thamesmead to the southeast of London. Its purpose was varied: to provide cool storage for product, particularly Easter Eggs which were stockpiled during the year for their short selling season; to house the distribution and storage functions from the soon-to-close Clarnico factory in Hackney Wick; and to provide a more spacious home for the fast-growing Moffat wholesale business at Maidstone and Camberwell in southeast London.

Celebrity endorsements

Sweet makers have always liked using celebrities to sell their products. With such tasty public exposure on offer, such stars soon swallow any concerns at diluting their credibility.

LEFT: it's unlikely Benjamin Britten always conducted with a jar of Extra Strong Mints beside his table, but he appeared to do so this time.

ABOVE: Ronnie Corbett at the height of his promotional powers for Moffat in 1971.

ABOVE: 'Half-ton Emlyn cheers 'em up!' screamed the headline as Emlyn Hughes, then captain of both England and Liverpool football teams, brought half a ton of Trebor sweets to children's hospitals. This was June 1979 – a time when few questioned equating children's health (and happiness) with unlimited piles of sugary sweets.

LEFT: Bob Monkhouse gets buried in toffees for Sharps in 1965.

RIGHT: pop star Dickie Valentine delights the Chesterfield staff when he arrives for a summer visit in 1955.

ABOVE: fag in hand, Max Bygraves enjoys a quick read of the Trebor Magazine, surrounded by Pat, Cicely, Ann and Beryl from the Chesterfield sample room in March 1957.

BELOW: yes, it's Philip Schofield, on the sofa with his booty bags in 1989.

ABOVE: Gary Lineker and John Barnes keep it up for Extra Strong Mints.

LEFT: what better way to express your devotion to those crazy Caledonian croonsters, the Bay City Rollers, than with these 1976 packs of chewing gum and picture cards?

ROYAL SUPPORT: Prince Philip (above) chats with a confectionery student at Chesterfield factory in 1959. The 1981 Royal Wedding (below) demanded tie-in products from virtually every manufacturer in the land.

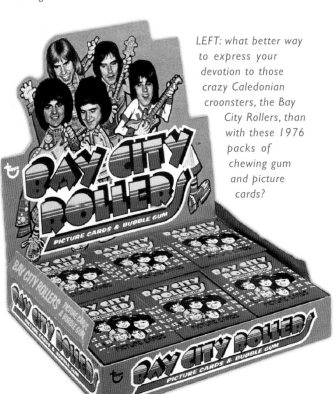

Opening up to consultants

The firm actively pursued outside opinion in exploring better ways to manage itself.

Ever since employing the wonderfully-named Institute of Industrial Psychology back in 1936, Sydney Marks was always keen to allow consultants deep into the firm and invite frank advice on how it should be run. Today this is commonplace, back then it was rare. During the late 1950s Sydney was attending a personnel management conference in the north of England when he was approached by a man called Warren Lamb, who persuaded him there was a science to making

The succession issue

Much debate and analysis surrounded the succession issue, particularly the roles that John and Ian Marks should take over from their father Sydney. In 1963 the management consultants Urwick Orr told Sydney he had three choices which, according to John Marks, were 'Go on until you drop, bring in professional managers, or see if your sons have any abilities.' He took the latter course, deliberately keeping the Sharps business separate and sending John to manage it in Maidstone.

In this, as in many decisions during the sixties and early seventies, Sydney relied on 'The Three Wise Men', a professional triumvirate comprising accountants Arthur Kearns and Clyde Dixie and lawyer Kevin Kennedy.

It's fair to say that the succession issue remained an issue of some intensity right up until the sale of the company in 1989. But this was not caused by any lack of insight. Indeed the Marks family showed courage in their repeated willingness to expose themselves to sharp personal scrutiny in their efforts to find the best way forwards.

people work better together. Lamb was invited to profile senior staff and match people with positions. Over the next decade Lamb's firm spent much time providing highly personal opinions on Trebor managers, not all of whom shared their boss's faith in the process.

Sydney Marks also sought outside economic advice. During the mid 1950s he got to know Professor Ronald Brech, who confidentially helped him develop five year plans for the firm. Brech remembers Sydney as 'a fascinating man – an instinctive businessman who made good decisions, but often without knowing why they were right.'

After Sydney Marks stopped running the business day-to-day, Trebor took a fresh approach to training management. Partly this stemmed from John Marks attending a course for senior executives at the American research university MIT in

Arthur Chapman joined Trebor in 1972 as personnel director. He was instrumental in setting up the firm's Organisational Development project and joined the board of Trebor Ltd before retiring in 1985.

1972. John had also got to know Harold Bridger of the Tavistock Institute of Human Relations in London and, through him, the writings of Rensis Likert, who encouraged more participative and supportive forms of management. In 1972 the group appointed a new personnel director: Arthur Chapman, who had pushed organisational change at the oil company Esso and was keen to put new thinking into practice. He in turn brought in a Dutch organisation called NPI (Netherlands Pedagogical Institute) and its UK manager Marjo van Boeschoten. They arranged a conference to discuss two current issues: high turnover of labour at Maidstone and tensions within the newly created customer services department.

In 1975 Chapman and NPI developed a week-long residential programme for each of the group's 350 managers and supervisors, representing over 10% of the workforce. Thirty at a time would head to the Down Hall conference centre in Essex – or later to Runnings Park near Malvern – for a week of discussion, exercises and lectures. By February 1977 when the programme finished, some 430 managers had taken part in what became known as the Down Hall experience. This represented a considerable investment in time and resource by the group. As Chapman later commented, 'It was a brave decision to spend £50,000 on organisational development in the middle of the cash flow crisis of the mid 70s. But it more than paid off.'

Management Today magazine commented on the Down Hall initiative in a May 1977 profile of the firm. 'Trebor is a significant but minor entity in a mature industry,' it concluded. 'Appropriately, therefore, much of management's energies are being directed towards maintaining the company's relative stability. In these circumstances, its essays in organizational development are a lot less indulgent than they might otherwise seem.' Despite the patronising tone, the journalist was actually praising the firm, and rightly so.

Harold Bridger and Marjo van Boeschoten continued to work with the firm over the next decade. Bridger helped the Marks family to manage succession issues while van Boeschoten, among other projects, worked with personnel director Jennifer Haigh to address equal opportunities for women.

Processing words...

TUCKED away in a corner of the first floor of Trebor House is a new machine which could revolutionise the production of customers' letters and reports. It is called a 'word processor'.

Basically, it functions like a typewriter with a video screen and a computer memory, and, without going into technical details, it can provide any number of documents automatically.

Sharon Crisp operating the word processor.

Above: in October 1979 Working Together revealed the new high-tech device that would transform the firm's communications: a 'word processor' which could eliminate the re-typing of reports and letters.

Below: Sydney Marks celebrated 60 years with the firm on 17th November 1978. Seen here at a party in the Forest Gate canteen are, from left, Alex Marks, John Marks, Sydney Marks, Bill Marks (son of John Marks) and Ian Marks. Despite retiring, Sydney kept an office in Trebor House. Bill Marks was one of the few members of the next generation of family to work with the firm.

Yvonne Avent remembers

'In those days Trebor was very enlightened. I said I had children and would have to have the school holidays and they agreed. I worked the hours that I wanted, half past nine to half past three, so I saw them off to school and was there when they came back. That happens a lot these days but not then – and that's how I came to stay.' Yvonne Avent joined the export department in 1967 and worked there until 1984.

Sweets of the 70s

Children remained the top target for Trebor during the 1970s, though the next decade was to see a leap in sweets for adults.

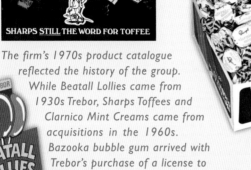

SHARPS STILL THE WORD FOR TOFFEE

The firm's 1970s product catalogue reflected the history of the group. While Beatall Lollies came from 1930s Trebor, Sharps Toffees and Clarnico Mint Creams came from acquisitions in the 1960s. Bazooka bubble gum arrived with Trebor's purchase of a license to make Topps products in Britain in the 1970s.

Right: kids have always loved sweet cigarettes. As Dylan Thomas wrote in *A Child's Christmas in Wales*: 'Ah! The packet of cigarettes: you put one in your mouth and you stood at the corner of the street and you waited for hours, in vain, for an old lady to scold you for smoking a cigarette, and then with a smirk you ate it.' *Above:* imagine selling kids today a 'Smoker's Outfit'.

Extra Strong Mints were popular both in weigh out and count lines.

Weigh outs not yet on the way out

Through the 1960s customers were keener to keep buying sweets by weight than the powers starting to control retail in the UK.

Supermarkets preferred countlines of branded products; quick, anonymous transactions were better for the bottom line. But many customers still preferred the old way of buying sweets – visiting a small shop, asking the shopkeeper to weigh out some goodies from a large jar and probably having some kind of conversation in the meantime.

This recalled a time when shopping was slower and more personal. As Nicholas Whittaker wrote in *Sweet Talk*, 'By the 1970s somebody could walk into a shop, buy a *Picnic*, *Mars* or a pre-packed bag of mints and depart without uttering a single syllable. But how many wanted such a life? As long as sweets maintained a psychological connection with affection, most people would still crave the human touch with their sweets.'

Trebor stood in the middle. The firm realised that branded goods were the way forward and spent huge sums to promote those brands. But by the late 1960s it still had thirty different weigh-outs and, through its distribution arm, dealt with the hundreds of thousands of small shops which still stocked the jars. Total brand domination was yet to come.

WATCH WITH MUMMiES

TREBOR ARE PUTTING THE FRIGHTENERS ON TV DURING MARCH AND APRIL. SHOWING NATIONALLY* DURING PRIME CHILDREN'S VIEWING TIME, THE LIGHT-HEARTED HORROR COMMERCIAL WILL REACH 80% OF CHILDREN AN AVERAGE OF 6 TIMES ..... AND TO MAKE SURE THEY ALL GET A TASTE OF THE TOMB, OVER ½ MILLION CHILDREN WILL GET FREE SAMPLES ON THE FRONT OF BUSTER, WHIZZER AND JINTY ON 19th APRIL.

Voiceover: Chilling tales of horror about some of the spookiest spooks around .....

Voiceover: You'll find them on the inside of every pack .....

Voiceover: ..... of new Trebor Mummies.

Spook 1: What's it say about you?
Spook 2: It says I'm a grisly spectacle.

Voiceover: And the sweets are just as creepy ..... fiendishly black, with hidden flavours ..... so you never know what to expect next .....

Mummy: Evening All!

Spook 1: 'Ere what's that?
Spook 2: Dunno ..... this place gives me the creeps!

Voiceover: New Trebor Mummies. A taste of the tomb.

Above and right: horror sweets have long been popular. Children loved heading down the newsagent to pick up some Munchy Maggots or Dead Men's Fingers. Trebor contributed to this trend with their Trebor Mummies 'the taste from the tomb', Terror Curses, Crawlies and Evil Eric Lollies.

Above: recent acquisition Clarnico gets equal billing with Trebor and Sharps at Christmas 1971.

Below and below left: the 1977 launch of Double Agents was a big one. Research-based flavours, a nationwide TV campaign – and some silly facemasks for the sales team.

Below: 1978 and Star Wars fever still rages across the land. Trebor Refreshers respond with 'May the fizz be with you'.

* 4 Exciting Flavour combinations based on latest consumer research
* Secret codes on wrappers
* Comprehensive national TV Campaign

More sweets of the 70s

Product launches became costlier and more complex as Trebor, like other sweetmakers, sought customer loyalty through comics, tv ads, competitions and giveaways.

Below: sweetmakers have long shared comics' love of silly words. This Treborland promotion featured 'Konks' and Robbers, with a belt of 'fantastic plastic' for only 75p.

Above: one shouldn't over-romanticise the 1970s. Top-selling Black Jacks were still marketed with lazily offensive imagery. Even Fumunchews (opposite page, top right) banked on a sloppy cultural stereotype.

Sugar and spice, and all that's nice

From an article in Working Together Summer 1973:

Sweets are sometimes called 'spice' and our Chesterfield factory is locally called 'The Spice Factory'. Schoolboys often invent their own names for sweets like 'sucks' or 'suckers'. We must like sweets as we, the British public, eat more sweets than anyone else in the world.

Some people eat sweets as an alternative to smoking, and Trebor Mints are the most popular sweet eaten for this reason. One office has a saying, 'A packet a day keeps a cough away.' Troops, too, have boiled sweets in their emergency packs as a compact quick source of energy for cases of exhaustion. But less than one twentieth of our average intake of calories comes from sweets and there must be very few cases where sweets are eaten as food. So we must be eating them then for pleasure.

In 1907 Trebor sold a 4lb jar of sweets for 10d, which sold in the shops at four ounces for one penny. In 1939 the same four ounces sold for tuppence, and by 1956 this had risen to sixpence. Today (1973) it would sell for twelve old pence. But though this price for sweets has doubled since 1956, wages have risen three and a half times. So sweets have become a lot cheaper over the years. Interestingly consumption is down. In 1954 the British consumed 9½ ounces per head each week, in 1972 this was 8 ounces. But it's still far ahead of other countries: Americans only each eat around five ounces per week.

Above: *Captain Hercules Hurricane was already a hero from the comic* Valiant *before he joined the pantheon of Trebor celebrity tie-ins. With his sidekick Maggot Malone, he here smashes the 'heartless huns' (World War Two german soldiers) on behalf of his Trebor chew.* **Above right:** *another comic tie-in were Fumunchews which traded off the success of martial arts TV shows such as Kung Fu and Hong Kong Phooey.*

Right and below: *Blobs featured a hard boiled exterior with a soft centre, and flavours 'you don't expect to find in a sweet' such as toffee apple and fizzy cider. Trebor launched them with their own storyline – a lad called Patch whose monster chums prefer to eat trash rather than the Blobs sweets he craves. Promotions included a competition to create disgusting menus for Chef Monster, stickers and free frisbees.*

Three year plan

Keen to grow – and needing to stay ahead – the firm embarked on its largest ever investment strategy.

In October 1976 *Working Together* announced plans to invest £15 million over the next three years in developing the group. 80% of this was earmarked for the UK, improving buildings, offices and equipment; the remaining £3 million would support overseas operations. To put this in perspective, the group now planned to spend, each year for three years, a sum one and a half times greater than its most recent annual profits.

It was a bold move, but a necessary one. None of the existing factories at Chesterfield, Maidstone, Woodford and Forest Gate could be seen as entirely modern facilities. Trebor needed to grow fast, just to stay ahead of its competitors in the second tier of UK sweet manufacture – Bassett and Barker & Dobson – let alone keep close to the chocolate giants of Cadbury, Rowntree and Mars. As a privately-held company, Trebor had always faced limited access to capital. Now it was determined to invest for growth.

The timing was good. By 1977 the price of raw cocoa had risen nearly 400% in a year, putting huge pressure on chocolate firms. Sugar confectionery remained a different market. It was fragmented, with few clear brand leaders and – compared to chocolate – was surprisingly underpromoted, with an advertising-to-sales ratio of less than 1.5%. Hence there was a good opportunity for bold investment.

Below: senior executives gather in November 1979. From left: Ted Gillespie, sales & marketing; JB Collins, chairman of Moffat; Ian Marks, managing director UK; George Kerr, manpower services; Arthur Chapman, personnel; Jack Thompson, later managing director Trebor UK; Arthur Sansome, central services; Peter Antonelli, technical; Allan Benn, overseas. Seated John Marks, chairman and Sydney Marks.

Colchester

May 1977 saw announcement of the main element in this investment: the group was to build a new £3 million factory at Colchester, close the Woodford factory and spend £1 million redeveloping that site into a new headquarters building. Colchester represented Trebor's first chance to create a plant from scratch, putting into action the new ideas for group working and devolved responsibility that managers had been exploring at Down Hall.

'The prospect of a new factory on a green field site,' explained one of the executives in charge of the project, 'offered an opportunity to put into practice what we had learned and also what we had been prevented from doing elsewhere by the constraints of space or tradition. We decided to organise people into small groups, each given a considerable level of responsibility for managing itself. In turn this meant that there could be a simple management structure with fewer levels.' Architects Arup Associates were hired to design and build the facility, while the group took care to ease the pain of closing the compressed tablet factory at Woodford. Consultant Lisl Klein, an expert in industrial psychology and a longtime collaborator with the firm, involved Woodford staff with planning the best possible layout for the new site.

Construction at Colchester started in 1978 with Niall Christie as works manager. It was a fast build. Production of *Trebor Mints* started on the site in 1980 and *Refreshers* in 1981. 1982 saw the shift of *Extra Strong Mints* production from Maidstone to a state-of-the-art automated line at the new facility.

Product and technical development

In 1978 the firm set up a department to develop new products. Previously it was up to individual brand managers to create fresh lines but now, with the three year plan demanding growth, it was time to co-ordinate the push into new markets. A particular target was the £600 million adult sugar market, towards which Trebor aimed with an array of products across boiled sugar, toffee, fudge and pressed lines such as *Trebor Mints* and *Refreshers*. 1980 alone saw six major launches: *Bon Bons, Fruit Salad* and *Black Jacks* stick packs, *Private Sweetly, Dandies, Coolmints* and *Simply Fudge*. Autumn 1981 brought *Softmints*, which were to become one of the firm's main success stories of the 1980s.

Meantime technical director Peter Antonelli was pioneering computer technology in making sweets. This included automating the *Extra Strong Mints* line at Maidstone, regulating its speed as necessary and checking flow rates for

adding ingredients such as mint oil. By 1981 Trebor claimed to be a leader in micro-processing within the confectionery industry; the *Refresher* plant within the new Colchester factory was totally automated. One of the aims of this effort, explained Antonelli, was 'to eliminate many tedious and repetitive tasks, releasing people for more interesting work.'

Right: *most Trebor packaging came from Printway, a specialist printers that was originally part of Sharps. From their premises in Maidstone, Printway produced cartons, labels and display cards for point of sale.*

A new look

Along with the investment of the late 1970s came a new branding for the group. When John Marks called in the image consultancy Wolff Olins to help, they first demanded an immersion in the running of the business. One of the consultants, Terence Griffin, was sent in to talk to Sydney Marks who, though retired, still kept an office at Trebor House. As Griffin recalled, 'He said, "Good morning", and I said, "Hello". Then he said, "I see you are a 'Hello' person. I'm more of a 'Good morning' person, but anyway sit down and I'll tell you anything you want to know."' Sydney went on to describe the business of making sweets: '"In the morning you buy sugar, lunchtime you make it into sweets and in the afternoon you sell it to the sweet shop. That's what we do here." He was presenting this incredibly simple trade and he as a simple trader and it was all very disingenuous because actually he was a very bright and clever man.' Woolf Olins went on to design the fluttering flag branding used across the Group.

The latter half of the seventies saw big leaps in group turnover. By 1977 total sales reached £121 million, nearly three and a half times the figure at the start of the decade, with profits up over five times. Growth steadied over the next few years as the £15 million investment plan started to kick in, but clearly Trebor greeted the 1980s in strong shape.

New logo: the fluttering flag helped cohere separate businesses within the Group, most notably Trebor, Moffat and Trebor Distribution.

Life back in the 1970s

In the February 1978 edition of the company magazine, Roger Benton told an unusual Christmas story. As area sales manager for Liverpool, he was stuck just before Christmas with a huge array of unsold festive product. His method for clearing it fast says something about life in Britain back then.

'With some 300 Christmas outers still to sell on December 20 we had a problem – who on earth were we going to sell them to? It so happens that on our trading estate we have three large factories. Most days street traders set up stalls outside the entrances to sell goods to the wealthy workers. So we thought, let's become street traders! But we may be contravening some trading law, says I. To be on the safe side, Larry Kenny went over to Huyton police station to explain our plan. He was told there was no objection, so long as we took our stock to the police station first to let them have a chance of purchasing some of the 'bargains'.

We promised that our estate car would be laden with goodies. In return we were promised that as many policemen as possible would be waiting for us. To achieve this end, notice of the 'sale' would be put out over their mobile radios.

This must have happened straightaway for ten minutes later police cars started arriving on our own forecourt. The result was that we sold a considerable amount of stock before we had even started to load the car. Eventually, armed with Christmas stock, a price list and a small cash float, we set off for the police station proper.

Imagine the scene – an estate car parked in the middle of a police station compound with the back door open. Christmas stock bulging out. Myself in a borrowed anorak, two sizes too big for me; Larry in a camel haired overcoat, frantically selling sweets to a growing queue of policemen. Fivers, tenners, one pound notes changed hands. Then the canteen ladies arrived, not only armed with purses and shopping bags, but also carrying two cups of tea for us.

Soon the queue and the stock had diminished. "Any more stock back at depot?" asked an excited inspector. "Yes," we replied. "OK, then load up and I'll take you to Kirkby Station." And so it went on all day. Our estate car was loaded up four times and went from one police station to another, ending up at Divisional Headquarters, where even the ADC bought a box of chocolates for his wife! On each visit we were given a police escort. Time was against us, it was getting dark and the only way we could get around to every station was to put our foot down. It's amazing how you are not stopped for speeding when the inspector's car is escorting you. And you know what? We sold out!'

Trebor Canada

As far back as 1927 Trebor sold its sweets in Canada through agents. In 1950 it set up its own distribution firm Trebor Confections, but its best success in the country only came in the 1970s when the firm set up Trebor Canada. Founded in Quebec province in 1972 after Trebor had taken over the locally-based Leeds Candy Corporation, this venture was notable for two reasons. Firstly, it built its own factory, a 60,000 sq ft facility in Granby, 50 miles east of Montreal. And secondly, unlike in most other markets, it sold mainly bagged product to supermarkets. Headed by William Letovsky and Ed Barr, Trebor Canada established a strong position for Trebor within this small, competitive market.

Confectioners Benevolent Fund

1978 saw the Diamond Jubilee of the Confectioners Benevolent Fund (CBF). Throughout those 60 years, Trebor and its people contributed generously to the fund, whose aim was to help those in distress who were working, or had worked, in the sweet-making industry.

Typical of the benefits offered by the fund at that time were paying someone's phone, heating or TV rental bills, or paying for them to go on holiday.

There were fund-raising committees throughout the firm, organising events such as film screenings, golf tournaments, race nights and christmas shows. Highly popular were the Candy Balls, still hosted to this day by the CBF's modern equivalent Sweet Charity. For many years the Candy Balls held a Candy Queen competition, and the company magazine eagerly featured the young women who competed for this honour.

Right: Candy Queen contestants featured regularly in the company magazine. In 1957 the London contest in Park Lane was won by Mrs Joan Smith (centre) from the samples room at Forest Gate.

Below: in 1977 Lesley Riches from South Wales won the top sales award. Trebor Salesmen of the Year were not asked by the company magazine to pose on the top of their new car.

Above left: Allan Hurndell joined Robertson & Woodcock in 1927 as a wages clerk. He went on to become the firm's buyer and, after serving in the war as a royal marine, pioneered the firm's ingenious by-passing of sugar rations during the late 1940s. After the acquisition of Sharps in 1969, Hurndell became group buying manager, finally retiring in 1974 after 47 years service.

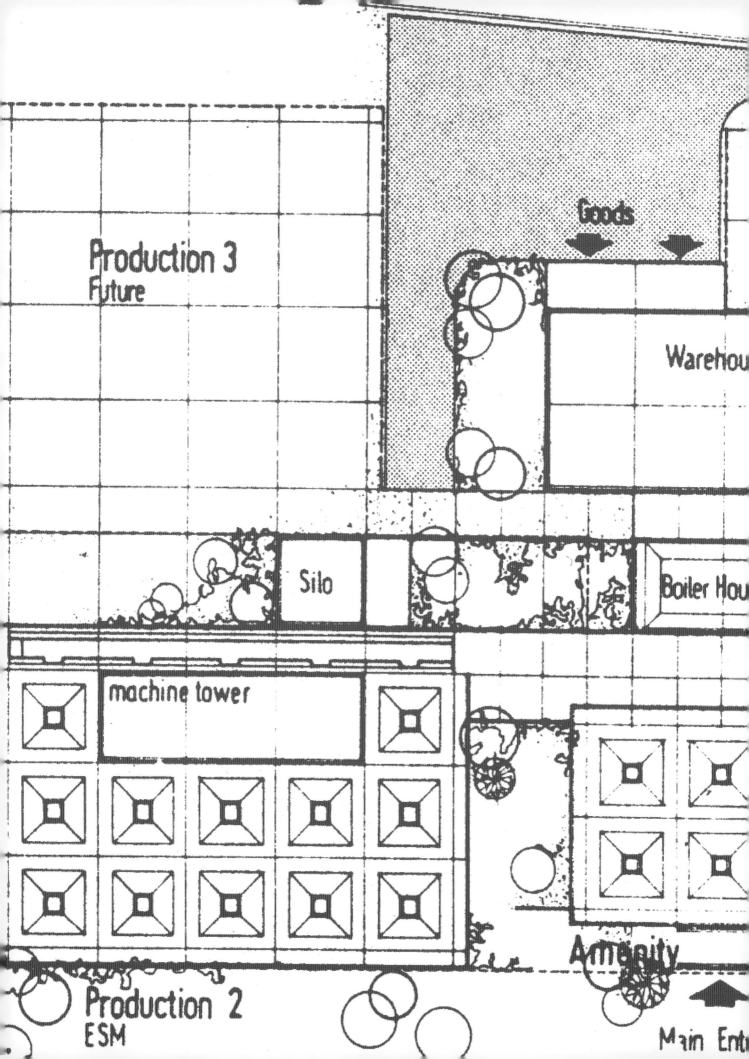

1980–1989

TOUGH AT THE TOP

With *Extra Strong Mints* racing out of the new factory at Colchester, Trebor now sold over half the mints bought in Britain. But such success raised the stakes. By the late 1980s it was harder than ever for a private family business to compete with global competitors.

Into the 80s

People now ate fewer sweets. Though Trebor led the field in children's confectionery, it needed more adult customers. The lure, it decided, was mints.

Below: after joining as an accountant in 1952, John Tibbles rose to become the group's financial director, retiring in 1984 to be succeeded by David Kappler.

Above: Gladys Weare joined the firm in September 1939, just as war started, and retired in 1983. As buying officer, she purchased raw materials, working for 34 years with Allan Hurndell then Clifford Broom.

1980 was a hard year for sweetmakers. The market was shrinking, thanks to competition from chocolate and crisps, a near doubling of VAT to 15% and a drop in the population of children. It didn't help that the UK was emerging from recession and the strong pound was playing havoc with exports. Trebor fared slightly better than its rivals, avoiding redundancies and three day weeks – and even achieving a 6% increase in sales to £135 million. In 1981 sales rose by 13% to £153 million. Trebor was now the UK's leading manufacturer of children's sugar confectionery, selling 2.5 million items every day.

But it was the largest slice of a shrinking cake. Sweet consumption continued to decline in 1981. Margins tightened and there was a risk the new capacity at Colchester might be superfluous. The directors realised they must gain yet more share, so the firm put more marketing effort into brands such as *Extra Strong Mints, Trebor Mints, Bonbons, Mint Imperials* and the new *Coolmints* and *Softmints* lines. The sales divisions continued to configure themselves around the growing power of supermarkets. So did Moffat, the firm's wholesaler of Trebor and non-Trebor products. Some 164,000 retail outlets needed servicing, so the sales teams were busy. Overseas the firm now sold over £20 million of sweets a year, both through exports and its foreign manufacturing companies. By 1982 the firm sold over half of all the mints sold in Britain. The marketing was working.

1983 saw significant changes in the firm's ownership when the Marks families arranged with many of the firm's smaller shareholders, often only distantly connected to the company, to sell their shares back to the group. This brought a further 38% of shares under the control of the families and helped the firm retain its independence as a family business. In 1984 the group divided itself into four separate operating companies, each with their own managing director as a director of the company. Jack Thompson headed Trebor UK, Frank Reed ran Moffat, Ted Gillespie ran Trebor International and Wallace Garland ran Trebor Group Distribution. Several non-executive directors came on board, including Don Angel, Tim Green and Peter Prior. They were joined by personnel director Arthur Chapman and finance director David Kappler, with Ian Marks as chairman and chief executive of Trebor Limited. John Marks remained chairman of Trebor Group Limited as well as a non-executive director with responsibility for external

affairs. As the 1980s progressed, the restructuring paid off. Profits rose by 40% in 1984, 25% in 1985 and a further 18% in 1986. Group sales now reached £299 million and, with the recent acquisition of Maynards, the firm was distinctly the largest sugar sweet manufacturer in the UK. While the overall market remained stagnant, Trebor had succeeded in its objective of raising share.

Overseas, the picture was generally strong. Japan and Ireland had started to perform well after a period of stagnation. So too Indonesia. Nigeria was profitable, though it remained difficult to get profits out of the country. The abiding weakness lay in the United States; all efforts to stem heavy losses there had failed so it was decided to close down operations and appoint a distributor instead.

Targeting adults

'Our old image as a manufacturer at the low-cost end of the market, especially in the children's market, has held us back in the past,' wrote Arthur Sansome, formerly the group chemist, in 1984. 'Changing to an adult image is the way forwards.' While Trebor had raised its share of the sugar confectionery market from eight to ten percent over the past six years, that market was declining steadily. Selling more sweets to adults might be a solution. As marketing director David Sowter said at the same time, 'The company now has more potential major adult brands than ever before.' He was referring to *Extra Strong Mints, Softmints* and *Imperials*. 'Rowntree is the only company which can match Trebor in the strength of its brands and promotional resources,' continued Sowter. 'Other companies without the brands and a strong salesforce have to cut prices and strike deals, and the retailer is then able to call the tune.' Another factor at play was the trend towards healthier eating, manifested particularly in concerns over the volume of sugar eaten by children. As Sansome said, 'We must continue to get away from the pure boiled sweet image and concentrate more on dairy ingredients – our *Nut Crunch* is a good example of a boiled sweet which has more than just sugar as flavour.'

This confectionery world was very different from earlier times, say the 1930s, when a manufacturer produced hundreds of lines which it then pushed into shops, which in turn would push them towards consumers. Now manufacturers limited their efforts to fewer brands, advertising them directly to consumers and hoping to generate such demand that retailers would feel compelled to stock them – and on terms advantageous to the manufacturer. By the 1980s it cost around half a million pounds to install production for a new line, but two million pounds or more a year to advertise and promote that line. Hence the reduction in lines and the growing power of the marketing teams.

Below: *Jennifer Haigh succeeded Arthur Chapman as personnel director when he retired in 1985. Previously manager of the Maidstone factory, she now led the firm's work to improve working conditions at all levels of the business. She was succeeded by Peter Wallace, who also came via Maidstone, and who stayed to manage the migration of staff after the sale to Cadbury.*

Above: *in 1984 Terry Spurling replaced Ted Gillespie as managing director of Trebor International. He joined Trebor in 1969 as an accountant and went on to run the firm's Indonesian factory before returning to oversee computerisation and then back to international operations.*

Left: *during the early 1980s Moffat developed its retail arm with Supershop – a chain of hundreds of newsagents who chose to operate under the Supershop banner. Here we see the 1986 opening of a Newcastle Supershop by Newcastle United and England football player Peter Beardsley (centre).*

Colchester opens

Four years in the making, the new Colchester plant was Trebor's first chance to create a factory from scratch, employing its best ideas for making sweets and improving conditions for staff.

On 26th June 1981 the Employment Minister Jim Prior came to open the new factory at Colchester. Production had already started on *Trebor Mints* and *Refreshers*, so the VIPs could see the new work practices in action. With no clocking in, no charge hands, one communal entrance and a restaurant shared by management and workers alike, this was a very different environment from that practised across most of Britain at the time.

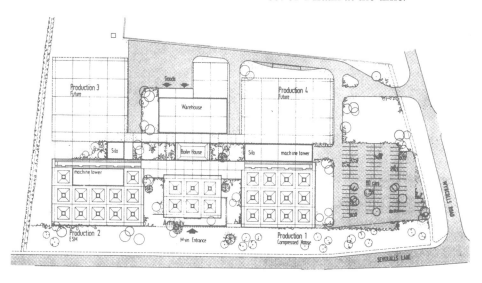

Above: aside from the new ways of working, Colchester was a large operation. This 94,000 sq ft plant aimed to produce 100 million rolls of sweet each year. It held 50 ton sugar silos for each of its three main lines: Refreshers, Trebor Mints and Trebor Extra Strong Mints.

Colchester reflected a strand of thinking that had long run through the firm, but been championed most energetically by John Marks during the 1970s – how to promote individuality and quality of life at work through greater participation and better industrial relations. The new facility aimed to be single status: management and staff shared a restaurant and car park, worked the same hours and received the same sick leave.

As Ian Marks said at the launch, 'We see the necessity to adapt to the changing needs of society, so we are trying to develop a management structure – and an environment – within the company which will enable it to cope effectively with change; an environment of mutual trust and respect.'

Arthur Chapman, the director of corporate development, explained the brief given to architects: 'Rather than an inhuman hangar concept, we wanted separate product 'houses' with which relatively small groups of people could identify. These are arranged around a central amenity area and energy centre and connected by a street.'

Below: the new Colchester factory was applauded for its humanity. Its redbrick construction, connecting smaller, connected spaces – mostly one-storey – contrasted with the vast windowless facilities typical of the day. Architects Arup Associates thought hard how to maximise daylight and provide warm social spaces within the building.

Sandy Brand, who was later brought in by Cadbury to support the transfer of processes to Sheffield, remembers Colchester being unlike any other factory. 'It felt like wherever you were, you could see outside,' she explains. 'Modern factories have no windows. Even today in Bournville the factory is largely dark. Windows tend not to be good in sweet production as people are tempted to open them.'

Staff were encouraged to take more responsibility, with operators trained to undertake basic maintenance on their machines. Each work group monitored its production and drew up its own work schedules; it also organised sending finished stock to the warehouse, maintained quality standards and trained new recruits. Rather than layers of line managers, there was only one product house manager on each production line, with teams left to solve as many problems as they could.

Technical director Peter Antonelli said at the launch, 'The building is pleasant to approach and is protected by careful landscaping. The almost constant awareness of the outside world, together with the gentle transition from the entrance through the "street" to the workplace, helps the view that work is part of life rather than a chore to be endured.'

Colchester went on to win two prestigious awards in 1983: the Premier Award from the Business and Industry Panel for the Environment and the Gold Award of the Royal Institute of British Architects. While the latter recognised the quality of building design, the former award also reflected the innovative approach to working conditions. There was even a model of the new factory on display at the Royal Academy's Summer Exhibition in 1981.

Above: staff at Colchester drew up their own work schedules, monitored production and even undertook basic maintenance on machines.

Assessing the success of the experiment

A special report in the Spring 1984 edition of Working Together addressed concerns from around the group that the 'anarchic' ways of working at the Colchester plant led to a lack of discipline. Niall Christie, the general works manager, explained they now had 36 months experience of the new work

Below: a Colchester work group plans the next week's job allocations with production engineer Frank Parkinson.

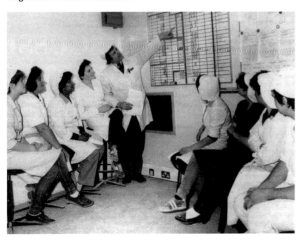

groups operating without traditional layers of supervision. 'We depend on everyone's self-discipline and self-motivation,' he explained, adding 'we have a strict disciplinary procedure. We average more verbal warnings than other factories because with the absence of first hand supervision we rely on the verbal warning to set people back on course.' But while the process was not always smooth, clear benefits were emerging. Sheffield University spent three years monitoring the plant and found that job satisfaction and commitment to the company were higher than ever recorded in British industry; absenteeism and labour turnover were among the lowest recorded. The experiment was succeeding.

Closure of two loyal factories

Progress comes at a price.

As the firm's new factory at Colchester started production, two of its longest standing plants came to close. Woodford, opened in 1949, helped drive post-war expansion, while Forest Gate was the firm's first home and produced sweets continuously for 76 years. Each was an important local employer, with some families sending several generations of worker to the same works. These closures were a great loss to their communities.

Above: an anguished look on the face of Helen Stephens as the last ever jar of sweets is filled at Forest Gate in 1983.

Woodford

29th January 1981 saw a party to say farewell to Woodford factory after 31 years of production. Alf Dixon, factory manager since the 1950s, shared some memories of how working there had changed. 'As the head office staff increased, so Trebor House expanded to take up more and more factory space. This meant we had to become more efficient in operation. It really helped when we changed from cut label roll-wrappers – 60 machines producing 380 sweets a minute each – to 13 rota-presses producing 3,000 sweets a minute each. But our most successful period has been the final 12 months of production, when we achieved 97% efficiency with a material loss of only 0.05%. And we assure you, there was no cooking of the books!'

Forest Gate

June 1982 brought the announcement that Forest Gate was to close during the next year. Ian Marks explained that the old plant could no longer be upgraded to a level required for modern production. Chews production would be transferred first, then high boilings for the home trade and finally export production. It was very sad to close production at the place where Ian Marks' grandfather and his three colleagues had first established the company – and to sever the firm's original links with the East End of London.

Naturally there were parties to celebrate Forest Gate's demise. There's a picture from one of them showing six women with, between them, 196 years of combined service at the factory. Vi Lee was the longest serving, having joined the firm in 1934. Twice during the war she was bombed out of the house where she lived, once being buried in the rubble for several hours. She

Right: six of the long-serving Forest Gate staff at the closing party in January 1983.

One hundred and ninety-six years' service between them! Front row, Vi Lee, Dolly Lamb and Mavis Lewis; Back row: Vi Lawrence, Ivy Brewster and Nell Antoine.

started in hand-wrapping, went on to finishing and then spent 21 years on the box-wrapping machine. Dolly Lamb had 35 years service, starting on a salary of £4 a week with a daily bonus of between two and five shillings. Vi Lawrence followed her mum Mabel into the factory in 1952 as a sugar feeder on the evening shift. Mavis Lewis worked 33 years, straight from school at the age of 15. Ivy Brewster started work 'on the belt', producing toffee bars called *Trumps*, while Nell Antoine joined Trebor soon after arriving from Jamaica in 1956.

Perhaps the greatest tribute to Forest Gate came from Sydney Marks in 1978 when celebrating his sixtieth year with the firm. 'It should give great satisfaction to pensioners and long-service employees,' he said, 'that at Forest Gate, on the site of an old tramway building and seven cottages, teams of people created the knowledge and knowhow to run four factories and 16 depots employing over 3,000 people in this country, five factories in different continents and other distribution businesses abroad.'

Death of 'Mr Sydney'

'It is with deep regret that we announce the death of Sydney John Marks, CBE, TD, Life President of the Trebor Group on Friday 12th December 1980' reported the company newspaper.

Two years earlier on 17th November 1978 he had celebrated his 60th year with the firm. His speech that day reflected his pride in what the company had become and is quoted several times within this book. He remained active after his Golden Jubilee, maintaining an office at Trebor House while his sons took leadership of the firm.

Unsurprisingly for a man of such initiative, Sydney Marks was always very active outside the firm. The army took up much of his spare time from the 1920s through to the 1940s. He served as president of the Cocoa, Chocolate and Confectionery Alliance from 1956-1959, president of the Confectioners' Benevolent Fund in 1952 and president of the International Sugar Confectionery Manufacturers' Association from

1972-1975. He was also master of the Tin Plate Workers livery company in the City of London. He loved sailing and served as commodore of the Blackwater Sailing Club in Essex.

But the centre of his life was Trebor. Son of one of the founding partners, Sydney Marks started influencing the business as soon as he joined in 1918. Within a few years he had spurred the mechanisation which helped the firm leap forward in the 1920s. Thenceforth his ambition, and vision, ensured the firm rose beyond its many competitors to become one of the great names of British confectionery.

Bill Deighan remembers
'Sydney John was an Eastender. That's what I think people saw in

him. Down to earth. We never had any need for unions at Forest Gate because the door was always open. If you had a problem there was always someone who could deal with it and sort it. Eastenders had the ability to argue one minute, but if there was any trouble, they'd help out in a flash. After Sydney retired he used to love joining the Forest Gate pensioner outings. He joined in all the singsongs in the coach – and he did that until he became too ill to go any more.'

Clifford Broom remembers
'Sydney Marks had parties thrown at every opportunity. Someone would tell him, Mr Sydney do you know we produced more tonnes last week than we've ever done before? Next thing you know, we're at the Savoy.'

Maynards

Trebor acquires another East London sweet firm.

In 1985 Trebor made one last major acquisition. As with Clarnico, it chose a well established name in confectionery, based in East London with a long history as a family business. Maynards was founded in 1896 by Charles and Tom Maynard, whose family had already been making sweets in their kitchen for several decades. In 1909 they launched their wine gums, which remain to this day an iconic brand of confectionery. Indeed, it was this strength in gums and jellies – especially the *Original Wine Gum* and the *American Hard Gum* – which attracted Trebor.

For £8 million the group acquired a sizeable facility in Tottenham, northeast London, with 450 people working in the Maynards factory, offices and warehouse. Along with the wine gums were a range of sweets for adults and children, including gums, pastilles and jellies, hard and soft sugar-coated lines and chocolate and coated bars. Trebor could now compete strongly in the pastille, gums and jellies sector, a traditional strength of its main rival Rowntree. Most importantly, Trebor was now the clear leader in sugar confectionery within the UK.

Above: *Maynards' product range prior to Trebor's takeover in 1985.*

Right: *Page Three pin up model Linda Lusardi arrives to award a trade incentive prize for Maynards wine gums to an excited newsagent couple. Her Edwardian costume reflects the introduction of Original Wine Gums in 1909.*

*Sweet production at the Vale Road Maynard factory in Tottenham included (**right**) hand-dipping Brazil nuts in maple fondant and (**above**) cutting the fudge.*

How sweets are made

All the sweets that we make come from a few basic ingredients which are treated in different ways to make different types of sweet. The main ingredients provide the bulk in the sweets. Other minor ingredients give flavour, colour and texture.

	Basic Ingredients
High Boiled	
Sherbet Lemons	Sugar
Chocolate Limes	Glucose
Low Boiled	
Toffees, Fudge	Sugar, Condensed Milk
Chews	Glucose, Fat
Mint Creams	
Jellies	Pectin (setting ingredient)
Chocolate	
Easter Eggs	Sugar, Fat
Buttersnaps	Cocoa Beans, Milk
Compressed & Lozenge	
Trebor Mints	Sugar
Refreshers	Gelatin
Extra Strong Mints	

High Boiled Sugar and glucose are heated to a very high temperature, and after cooling somewhat the mass is coloured and flavoured. It is then further cooled until it has the consistency of plasticine, and put through a machine which moulds the individual sweets at a rate of over a ton per hour. It also cools them until they are hard. They are then taken to wrapping machines to be wrapped in various ways.

Low Boiled Sugar, glucose, condensed milk and fat are heated to lower temperatures than the high boiled sweet mixture. The cooked mass is cooled and either poured into slabs for later cutting or, after cooling to the consistency of plasticine, put into machines which can cut the sweets to shape and wrap them at the same time.

Mint Creams Sugar and glucose are boiled, cooked and beaten to make the sugar form very tiny crystals. This creates a paste which is flavoured, shaped and then soaked in sugar syrup to form a sugar crystal coat, which prevents the sweet drying out and going hard.

Jellies Sugar and glucose are boiled, and pectin is added. After colouring and flavouring, the mix is poured into depressions in a bed of starch powder and allowed to set.

Chocolate A mixture of chocolate crumb (cocoa beans and milk), sugar and warm fat is ground together to form a liquid, the consistency of custard. This is then pumped to where it can be used, either to make shapes like Easter Eggs, or to cover toffees or bars, eg Buttersnap.

Compressed Tablets & Lozenges These are made from icing sugar and gelatin, suitably flavoured and coloured. No cooking takes place. Compressed sweets are stamped out by punches and are immediately ready for wrapping. Lozenge sweets are cut out of a moist dough-like mixture, and are left for 48 hours to dry in an oven before wrapping.

So there it is – the wide range of confectionery manufactured by the Company comes from relatively few major ingredients cooked, shaped and packed in different ways.

Right: Wallace Garland joined the firm in 1984 to head up Trebor Group Distribution (TGD). Managing 700 people, mostly in the firm's depots nationwide, he brought efficiencies to the way goods were carried and stored. TGD primarily served the firm's Moffat wholesaler, but also distributed product for companies such as Wrigley and Threshers.

Distribution

Much of the firm's turnover during the 1970s and 1980s came from wholesaling goods from both Trebor and elsewhere, especially cigarettes. As a result, the firm's twelve distribution depots featured often in Working Together, the company magazine.

In the summer of 1985 the magazine profiled the depot at Hoddesdon, northeast of London. This depot's history was typical of the firm's amalgamation of smaller, local wholesalers into the Moffat empire. It was set up in 1972 to handle the business of Betsers in Waltham Abbey, Gardiners of Ipswich and Frosts of Kings Cross. Fifteen drivers delivered goods across East Anglia, Essex, Hertfordshire, Middlesex and London.

The warehouse stocked more than 550 different types of cigarette, cigar or pipe tobacco, all under the eye of tobacco manager Gus Gale. 'Now that the average pack price of cigarettes is £1.25, Gus looks back to the earlier era of 20 Players for one shilling and ninepence.' There was a Moffat sales team on site, with both telesales and travelling reps.

Typically for the firm at this time, many families had several members working at the same place: for example, Janet Clark is a warehouse assembly supervisor while her son Richard drives the fork-lift truck on Goods In. And typically for a Working Together profile, there's mention of food: 'The specialty of Jena Lane, canteen manager, is her bread pudding. The secret of her success is her new microwave oven!'

Above: same job, different continents. Trebor drivers in the UK and Indonesia pose before their vehicles.

Above: warehouse staff at the Moffat's Manchester Depot perform a knees-up for the company photographer in 1983. Possibly the woman on the right didn't get the memo about unconfined jollity.

It's not easy to run a sweet firm

John Middleton started as an accountant at Chesterfield factory in the early 1970s, before taking a series of management positions around the firm. Here he describes some of the challenges of supplying popular sweets nationwide.

'Imagine Mrs Bloggs has a cornershop in Bath and she's run out of *Black Jacks*. She tells her local Trebor salesman who orders more stock to be delivered to her. His order is collated with other orders from his depot in Devizes and sent through to head office where it's combined, overnight on the main frame computer, with orders from the firm's twelve other satellite depots around the country. The demand is matched with current stock levels. Ideally there is sufficient stock of *Black Jacks* in the Devizes depot to go on the weekly truck that visits Mrs Bloggs' shop. If there isn't, then she doesn't get her *Black Jacks*, but she does get the salesman from rival distributors Swizzells coming round – who can supply *Black Jacks* and other goods beside. So Trebor loses the order.

There are many reasons why the depot could not supply to her. Maybe Devizes had not ordered enough from the bulk depot at Thamesmead. Or there'd been more demand than usual for *Black Jacks* that month and the supply from Chesterfield factory had run out. Or there had been hitches in the distribution at any stage in the chain. Whatever the reason, the sale has been lost. Lose too many such sales and the business declines.

Ideally each depot would always have enough stock for any eventuality. But demand fluctuates and stock goes off. In any case it's unwise to tie up too much capital in unsold stock. So how do you balance this equation?

The answer lies in accurately predicting future demand – and knowing what might affect this demand. If, say, the firm is planning a promotion, then sales of *Black Jacks* might rise by 20%. Or a competitor might launch a similar product which eats into *Black Jack* share. Or the firm might launch a product which cannibalises *Black Jack* sales, or a sales incentive on another product might make salesmen avoid *Black Jacks* for a while. With this number of variables, you must try to control as many as possible. The management skill for a business like Trebor was to make sure everyone in the firm spoke clearly to each other.'

TREBOR
1986
LOCATIONS

GLASGOW

BELFAST

LEEDS

MANCHESTER

CHESTERFIELD

MANSFIELD

WALSALL

NORTHAMPTON

COLCHESTER

HODDESDON

NEWPORT

WOODFORD

BRENTWOOD

TOTTENHAM

DEVIZES

THAMESMEAD

MAIDSTONE

HASLEMERE

● DEPOT
● FACTORY
● OFFICE

Sweets of the 80s

While the Trebor range remained diverse, the success of *Softmints* and *Coolmints* heralded the rising dominance of mints within the brand.

ABOVE: 1984 saw the arrival of a new Trebor logo. The fluttering flag-style banner, introduced in 1977, was not felt to be popular with the public, and was technically difficult to print on small packs. The new, simpler banner first appeared on Pick 'n Mix and was then rolled out across the firm's products.

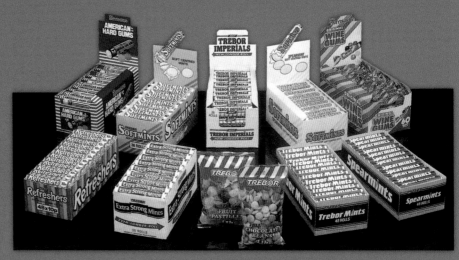

ABOVE: the headline brands of 1986 included old favourites like Trebor's Extra Strong Mints, Refreshers and Imperials alongside the newly acquired Maynards Wine Gums and American Hard Gums. Eighties newcomers Softmints have settled in well, along with the 1984-launched Spearmints. Fewer boiled sweets feature as mints take over. By now the firm was installing Mint Bars in shops to make the most of its range.

ABOVE: Devon Candies was a small manufacturer in southwest England which for several years had supplied fruit jellies to supplement those produced at Maidstone. The jellies were a popular component to the Pick 'n Mix range. After the acquisition, Trebor switched all jelly production to this specialist supplier.

ABOVE: Coolmints, the firm's first sugar-free mint, were launched in the summer of 1980. Demand for sugar-free confectionery had grown massively in the US and Europe through the late 1970s, but there were delays before Trebor could join the market. Many problems arose from learning how to use the ingredient Sorbitol, which needed air conditioned facilities to stop absorbing moisture. Delays in completing the Colchester factory meant production was set up in Chesterfield. Coolmints were packed in 14s, in an ice-blue wrapper and sold for 10p per roll.

RIGHT: since the 1950s Trebor sold chocolate sweets from another sweet firm in northeast London, the Tottenham-based Jameson's. Best known for their Raspberry Ruffles, Jameson's also turned out speciality lines like the Knock Out chocolate covered coconut bar.

Bet you can't get to the next roundabout before you have another Softmint.

LEFT AND BELOW RIGHT: introduced in 1981, Softmints remain a very popular sweet. With their hard peppermint shell and chewy interior, these mints do not simply dissolve slowly in the mouth. You can hurry their eating, and quickly start another – an advantage emphasised in the early print ads. Spearmint Softmints appeared later. This wonderful TV ad from 1987 (below) featured a musical pastiche of the band The Cure, with the words 'Oh Mr Soft can you tell us why the world in which you live in is so straaaange ... so soft and re-arraaaanged.'

SOFTFRUITS: these arrived in 1986 to build on the two other 'softees' Softmints and Spearmint Softmints. With their crisp shell and chewy centre containing natural fruit juice, Softfruits were aimed at both adults and children.

A Day in the Life of Norman Normal.

1. Open on Norman Normal, an ordinary little chap, setting off to work from his ordinary little house.

2. NORMAN: Here we go, another uneventful day. Nothing out of the ordinary ever happens to me.

3. ...I wish life was as varied as these new Trebor Dandies. Mmm, a Sherbet Lemon.

4. There are so many different sweets and flavours...

5. ...in a roll of Dandies you never know...

6. ...what to expect next!

7. Well, what a surprise! Choc flavoured Lime.

8. The variety of Dandies never ceases to amaze me!

Voice Over: New Trebor Dandies. As varied as life itself.

Heavyweight TV Campaign, equivalent to £850,000 at national level, will mean Dandies commercials being seen day after day in peak viewing time, for 15 weeks of the year.

DANDIES: from Chesterfield emerged the new line Dandies, a high quality high boil sweet with four different fruit and sherbet centres. It was advertised with the help of animated character Norman Normal.

1989–2012

SALE & BEYOND

Once sale became inevitable, the family sought to steer the firm into safe hands. They sold to Cadbury. But two decades later, Cadbury was swallowed up by Kraft Foods.

Selling the firm

As the 1980s came to a close, it became harder for a private business, even a strong one, to match the might of global competitors.

Few family firms survive the passing of their founders – and fewer still outlive the second generation. Yet Trebor survived, and thrived, with its third generation. Technically it was not always a single family firm, but in effect it soon became run by the Marks; and gradually this control became reflected in the shareholding, especially after the buyback of many smaller shareholders. By this stage the firm was led by Ian and John Marks, the third generation. As a family business, it was clearly very successful. But would the fourth generation wish to take their place at the helm?

Between the families of Ian and John Marks, and their sister Diana, there were nine children. Two of them spent time with the firm: Ian's daughter Caroline worked in marketing, while John's son Bill worked with Moffat. This was different from previous generations. Ian and John both started with Trebor during their school holidays and were expected to join the business full-time. Their father Sydney and uncle Alex similarly entered the firm as soon as possible.

Family businesses exert many of the psychological pressures of, say, stately homes.

But though the fourth generation – known within the family as G4 – were not forced behind a desk at Trebor House, they were expected to learn how the firm was run. They attended briefings with the heads of each department. They met with Harold Bridger, the industrial psychoanalyst from the Tavistock Institute who had long worked with the firm's senior management. Even if they did not wish to work for Trebor, they were being trained to make informed decisions about its future.

Selling the firm, or taking it into public ownership, was by no means obvious. Family businesses exert many of the psychological pressures of, say, stately homes. One is expected to preserve and pass on what one has been bequeathed; generations are reluctant to be known for losing or cashing in the inheritance. Yet commerce is different from landed property. There were changes afoot within the sweet industry which made Trebor's future as a family business more precarious.

Rowntree falls
In June 1988 Nestlé bought Rowntree for £2.5 billion. This great British Quaker firm – the fourth largest chocolate-maker in the world after Cadbury, Mars and Hershey – was swallowed by the Swiss giant, the world's largest food company. There was outrage over the sale of a major, healthy British firm to a foreign buyer, an event then unusual in Britain, but Thatcher's government was happy to open the door, letting the sharp wind of short-term capitalism blow away the less easily realisable benefits of established, indigenous industry.

That said, Rowntree had been an aggressive competitor to Trebor. It had recently launched *XXX Mints* as an obvious spoiler to challenge the market-leader *Extra Strong Mints;* the Trebor directors consulted trademark counsel over the possibility of litigation, but decided the case was not worth pursuing.

With Nestlé backing competitive lines like *XXX Mints*, Trebor's *Extra Strong Mints* and *Refreshers* were now up against brands with global reach and deep marketing pockets. It was hard for a relatively small private business to compete on such a scale. This was exacerbated by the buyback of small shareholders; by reducing shareholders' capital, the buyback also lessened the company's capacity to borrow; at the same time, it increased the firm's borrowings on top of the debt still around from building the factory at Colchester. Turnover remained healthy, the firm remained fit, but the combination of greater debt with lesser borrowing capacity limited the directors' scope for fresh investment. It could be argued that, so long as the Marks family wanted to keep tight, personal ownership of the firm – maintaining altruistic traditions of ownership unthinkable in a publicly quoted business – the resulting lack of investment capital would make growth, and long-term survival, untenable.

This came to a head as the confectionery industry continued to convulse through the late 1980s. Bassett was struggling and open to bids. Though smaller than Trebor, the northern-based Bassett was a significant player within sugar confectionery. In the mid 1980s the Swedish firm Procordia made a bid for Bassett, but Bassett chose instead to approach Trebor. The fit looked strong – together they could dominate sugar confectionery and challenge the might of the chocolate giants. But for various reasons, including the potential difficulty of borrowing enough money, Trebor decided not to bid.

Cadbury

Instead, Ian Marks suggested to Cadbury Schweppes that it buy Bassett. This other great Quaker chocolate-maker was upset not to have got its own hands on Rowntree, so creating a world-beating British chocolate giant. It was also fighting off an opportunistic attack by the US firm General Cinema, which had amassed nearly a fifth of its shares. Cadbury Schweppes needed to grow and build its independence. One obvious route lay through expanding into sugar.

Cadbury Schweppes had long wanted more share of sugar sweets, partly for growth and partly to gain greater control of retail display during the summer when chocolate sales dropped and the powerful supermarkets shifted from chocolate to sugar sweets and chewing gum. Having failed to launch several sugar products such as *Trillions* and *Tops*, it realised the best path was to buy

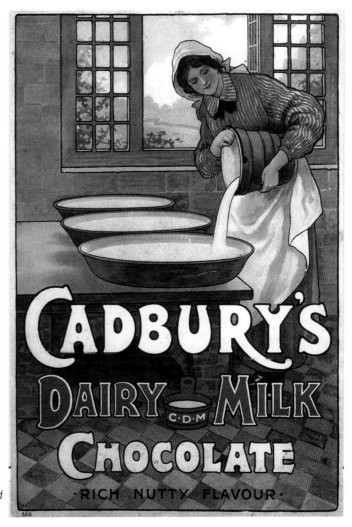

Right: founded in 1824 by the Quaker John Cadbury in Birmingham, this family chocolate firm soon grew to become one of the great names in European confectionery. Dairy Milk arrived in 1905, with a glass and a half of milk in each half pound bar.

Trebor's position within sugar confectionery

These three charts from the 1989 Information Memorandum gave bidders for Trebor some insight into the firm's strength, relative to its competitors.

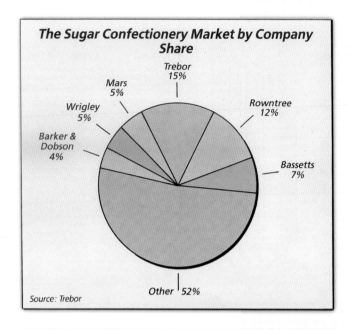

The Sugar Confectionery Market by Company Share

Trebor 15%
Mars 5%
Wrigley 5%
Barker & Dobson 4%
Rowntree 12%
Bassetts 7%
Other 52%

Source: Trebor

Left: you can here see Trebor's leading 15% share within the sugar confectionery market. The named brands were steadily taking share from the largely unbranded Other sector. Cadbury wanted to enter and dominate this market. It bought Bassett and held some Other share through owning the small Lion Confectionery and through its own *Chocolate Eclairs* and *Murray Mints*. But Rowntree was out of reach, owned by Nestlè. When Trebor came into play, Cadbury could not let someone else snap it up. They had to bid.

Below left: this shows the different categories of sugar sweets, and their relative market size.

Below: some product types were more important than others. Bassett dominated Liquorice hugely with its *Allsorts*, but (as the chart on the left shows) this was a small sector. Similarly, Mars dominated Chews with *Opal Fruits* and Medicated with *Tunes* and *Locketts*, but these sectors were also relatively small. Traditionally leading sectors such as Boiled Sugar and Toffee were in decline. The future lay in softer eating – in pastilles, mints and chewy sweets – where Trebor had strongest potential.

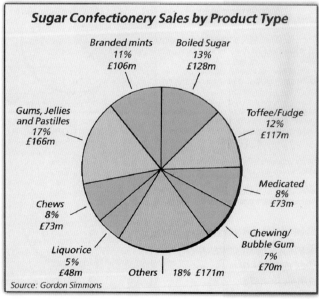

Sugar Confectionery Sales by Product Type

Branded mints 11% £106m
Boiled Sugar 13% £128m
Gums, Jellies and Pastilles 17% £166m
Toffee/Fudge 12% £117m
Medicated 8% £73m
Chews 8% £73m
Chewing/Bubble Gum 7% £70m
Liquorice 5% £48m
Others 18% £171m

Source: Gordon Simmons

Company Shares by Product Type

Product	Trebor	Rowntree	Bassetts	Mars	Cadbury
Boiled Sugar	2	0	0		0
Toffee/Fudge	1	1			2
Branded mints	4	3			
Pastilles	2	3	1		
Chews	1			4	
Liquorice	0		4		
Medicated				4	
Others	1		1		

0	1	2	3	4

under 5%, 5 – 10%, 11 – 30%, 31 – 40%, over 40%

Source: Gordon Simmons

existing competitive brands. It started with northern manufacturer Lion Confectionery in 1988, then it bought Bassett Foods the next year. Now *Jelly Babies* and *Liquorice Allsorts* were within the Cadbury fold.

Ian Marks had encouraged Cadbury to buy Bassett, thinking they might then need to come and make an offer for Trebor, so cementing their strength in sugar sweets. He had approached them privately, already believing the firm may well need to be sold.

Though the Bassett takeover didn't take place until 1989, the potential implications had hung over Trebor for several years beforehand. During this time the G4 generation of the Marks family met regularly by themselves, facilitated by the management academic Charles Handy and his artist wife Elizabeth, and occasionally with their parents, who were known as G3. They continued their briefings with company executives. Discussions centred around G4 representation on the board of the holding company, but it was becoming apparent that Trebor would have trouble surviving in its private form. The first person to raise the subject of selling the firm within a family meeting was John and Ian's older sister Diana; she later described this breaking of the ice as both a relief and a shock. Once the subject was raised, its logic became clear. By early 1989 the G4 group were convinced of the need to sell. They told their parents, who agreed.

David Kappler *worked at Cadbury before becoming Trebor's finance director. After the sale he rejoined Cadbury where he later became chief financial officer.*

The sale

Cadbury Schweppes did make an offer, but Trebor's group structure required a process of public bidding. Lawyer Charles Woodhouse started organising the sale in March 1989, instructing Arthur Andersen to create the necessary documents for bidders. There were plenty of suitors, from the German-Swiss confectioner Jacobs Suchard to the US tobacco giant Philip Morris. (Interestingly, Philip Morris had bought Kraft Foods the previous year and in 1989 acquired Suchard). Yet most people considered Cadbury Schweppes the chief contender. Trebor's finance director David Kappler still had many contacts within Cadbury from his years working for the firm.

A public offer duly came from the headquarters in Bournville. While the offer was not high enough, Trebor knew that the Moffat wholesale operation would have to be divested before the firm could be sold. An attempted management buy-out did not work, even on generous terms offered by the family, so Moffat went to rival wholesalers Palmer & Harvey.

Trebor was sold to Cadbury Schweppes for £146 million. £26 million paid off debts. Of the remaining £120 million (before tax), £99 million went to shareholders, who were mainly family, and £21 million went to past and present employees via the Orchid Fund (see separate box for details). Cadbury Schweppes merged its newly acquired sugar confectionery operations to form Trebor Bassett Ltd which it sought to operate separately from its main chocolate business.

Niall Christie remembers

'Because of the rules on insider information everyone was sworn to secrecy, but everyone knew something was going on. Odd things happened, like we'd be asked to do a stock check on all our machinery spare parts – something we'd had never done before because they were written off as soon as we bought them. So that's obviously pricing up the company isn't it? Strange visitors came, like an American guy who was associated with Hall's Menthol-lyptus. He comes and has a walk around, but his walk around is a bit more detailed than usual.' Niall Christie was works manager at Colchester factory.

The sale, when it came, came quickly. Even though the acquisition had to be cleared by the Office of Fair Trading, it was formally signed on 1st November 1989. The day before signing, John and Ian Marks hosted an informal farewell in the canteen at Trebor House.

In a letter to employees, John and Ian Marks wrote, 'With the acquisition of Rowntree by Nestlé, then Bassett being acquired by Cadbury, it was time for a review of where our future lay. A family business thinks last about losing its identity so the first step was to see whether some alliance could be formed without losing our independence. It soon became clear that an alliance would be in name only and we would be junior partners. This was not in our nature. So then the search was on for the best home for Trebor. In Cadbury we found a British company that treats its employees well, has a wonderful name, and also has a new-found interest in the sugar confectionery industry.'

Above: visit the old Cadbury headquarters at Bournville in Birmingham and you will find, even today, sturdy reminders of the Quaker family's dedication to improving the lives of their workers. A cricket pitch still abuts the Kraft Foods factory. Greenery infuses the utopian dwellings of Bournville Village, a model community started in the 1890s. By 1919 doctors were finding Bournville children to be on average 2-3 inches taller and eight pounds heavier than those from poorer parts of the city.

The Orchid Windfall

One of the more unusual aspects of the firm's sale was the generosity of the family to its employees past and present.

Of the £120 million realised after debts were paid, but before tax, the Marks family decided to allocate £21 million to staff. As John Marks explains, 'Our father Sydney was absolutely committed to staff sharing in any profits we made. So of course they should share in our profits at selling the company.'

Clifford Broom had the task of allocating what was known as the Orchid Fund. He assessed what each employee should receive, depending on their position and length of service. A shopfloor worker with five years service got a bonus of 50% of their annual salary; this rose to 100% for 25 years service. Even someone who had only spent one year with Trebor received a 25% bonus. Orchid also included many people who had already left the firm, who received a hike in their pension, plus a lump sum to backdate this to their retirement. The letters arrived a few days before Christmas.

£3 million went to staff overseas, with unexpected payments arriving through letterboxes as far afield as Lagos, Jakarta, Sydney and Johannesburg.

Niall Christie, manager at Colchester factory, remembers the afternoon when the announcement was made. 'People on the shop floor were invited into the office by the manager and told what they were going to receive. Someone who had been there only ten months got a thousand quid, a huge sum in those days. Those who'd worked longer got much more. Everyone sat around speechless. It was beyond their wildest dreams. They were thinking, this'll pay for a holiday, buy a car, pay off the mortgage, settle my debts. They thought Christmas had come ten times over. It was a wonderful, wonderful afternoon. We didn't get a lot of work done, but I'll never forget it. I wasn't surprised the family did it, but I was surprised at the scale of what they gave.'

In the Trebor Archive, there's a thick file of thankyou letters from gobsmacked pensioners. George Woollard of Forest Gate was delighted with the 'unexpected but very much appreciated gift.' During 32 years as a factory engineer, 'the work was hard and the hours long, but I was always made to feel part of the company rather than just a clock number.' He'd intended to put his gift into savings, but 'to hell with it, I'm 69 and probably haven't got all that much time to go, so I've booked a holiday in Spain for my wife and I.'

Ida White of Maidstone said, 'when I received the monthly pension slip, I thought there had been a mistake,' while Dorothy Hawkins in Chesterfield was delighted her monthly pension was rising to £30.58.

The Marks family has since maintained the generosity it showed with Orchid. In their low key way, the descendants of Sydney Marks have practised wide and thoughtful philanthropy. They continue to do so.

Saying goodbye: *John and Ian Marks stand beside the portrait of their father Sydney at Trebor House on 31st October 1989. They had just hosted a farewell party in the canteen. The next day, 1st November, Trebor officially became part of Cadbury Schweppes.*

In new hands

What happened to *Extra Strong Mints*, *Softmints* and the other Trebor brands after the shift in ownership to Cadbury and then Kraft Foods?

In late 1989 Trebor employees received a personal letter from their new boss – John Sunderland, managing director of Cadbury's freshly-created Sugar Confectionery Division. Sunderland was later to become chairman of Cadbury itself, but his task then was to merge the new acquisitions of Trebor, Bassett and Lion with Cadbury's own sugar business. Worried staff may not have been reassured by the opaque language – 'we are looking at how we will integrate our systems', 'how can we best use the manufacturing capacity we have at our disposal and plan to become a lower cost business competitively?', and 'should our head office be in Sheffield, Woodford Green or some other site?'.

Sunderland was now responsible for a stellar line-up: *Trebor Extra Strong Mints, Trebor Mints, Sharp's Toffee, Maynard's Wine Gums, Murray Mints, Bassett's Liquorice Allsorts* and *Bassett's Jelly Babies*. Trebor Bassett, as the division became known, was instantly the largest name in British sugar sweets, with twice the share of its nearest competitor Rowntree/Nestlé. Later in 1996 Trebor Bassett acquired brands Barker & Dobson, Butterkist, Keiller and Craven's of York.

During the 1990s Cadbury kept this sugar business separate from its main chocolate firm. This was mainly for marketing reasons: if merged straightaway,

Top Selling UK Sweets 1991

Following its formation in March 1990, Trebor Bassett held a market share twice that of its nearest competitor Rowntree/Nestle in the sweet (not chocolate) market. Here, marked in red, were its brands among the UK's top 20 sweets.

Some chocolate products from Cadbury now came under the Trebor Bassett name, along with Pascall favourites such as Murray Mints.

1	Rowntree Fruit Pastilles
2	Trebor Extra Strong Mints
3	Rowntree Polo Mints
4	Mars Opal Fruits
5	Trebor Softmints
6	Mars Tunes
7	Wrigley's Orbit Gum
8	Bassett's Liquorice Allsorts
9	Cadbury's Chocolate Eclairs
10	Mars Lockets
11	Maynards Wine Gums
12	Leaf Chewits
13	Rowntree Fruit Gums
14	Halls Mentho-lyptus
15	Bassett's Jelly Babies
16	Wrigley's Spearmint Gum
17	Rowntree Triple X
18	Warner Lambert Clorets
19	Trebor Mints
20	Mars Skittles

Merging factory cultures

Factories develop characters of their own, especially within a firm like Trebor which prized familial relationships and long service. But when ownership changes, factories close and production moves, those cultures become tested.

TREBOR BASSETT

Gary Carcary was taken on as a quality control manager at the Maidstone factory in February 1990, soon after it was taken over by Cadbury. 'Though it was behind the times in terms of quality operating principles, Maidstone made a high standard of products. You could tell it had a family environment – it was a cosy place with long established managers and often members from the same family working there. It featured what we called a "pocket book process", whereby a lot of production knowledge was housed in people's heads or in a book they kept in their pocket. Chesterfield was similar: very traditional, family-oriented and based on old processes. But Colchester was different, which was hardly surprising as it was modern and purpose-built, modelled on best practice with a linear flow on one floor and younger, flatter management. It was leaner, but bland, with little of the character of the other factories.'

Keith Newton joined Trebor Bassett in 1992, working at Colchester and Maidstone. 'In 1995 Colchester still firmly held its old Trebor culture, an odd mix of a flat structure with people empowered to make decisions but without a great sense of accountability. Volumes of *Extra Strong Mints* were down from 9,000 tons at their height to 4,500 tons; it felt like a product in decline. At Maidstone, Cadbury invested strongly in *Softmints* during the mid nineties, bringing nearly a third more volume on site. It also brought in Colchester-style structures, giving more technical skills to operators rather than maintaining a separate technical division.'

Sandy Brand joined the Maidstone technical department in the late 1990s as a technical information manager, supporting the transfer of production up north as each of the Trebor factories closed. As she explains, 'There's a black magic to sugar craft. It took us a long time to make *Extra Strong Mints* work in Sheffield. This was unexpected. None of the experts from Colchester came up to work the new line, which we hadn't thought would be a problem as the old-fashioned machinery still worked and the process looked straightforward. In any case, I'm not sure the experts themselves knew how they had made the sweets. We had to learn all over again and it took us a year. For example, we tried all sorts of equipment to dry the mints, even pasta dryers. But we got there in the end.'

Above right: March 2000 saw the £4.5million launch of Mighty Mints, a mini version of the Extra Strong brand. This aimed to match the appeal of rival mini mints, such as Smint and Polo Supermints, among young adults. Months later the product was redesigned after people noticed it looked very similar to pills of class A drug Ecstasy. In 2004 they changed their name to Mini Mints.

then the Cadbury salesforce were likely to focus on the chocolate best sellers and treat sugar products as second class citizens. Moreover, Cadbury planned to increase prices and profitability. For example, *Trebor Extra Strong Mints* sold for 20p per roll at the time of the sale; within three years that price nearly doubled. Having acquired all these brands, some competing with each other, Cadbury also needed to identify the strongest brand in each line and close or sell the weaker ones. Moreover, a corporation the size of Cadbury had less patience with smaller product lines; they were simply not worth the marketing cost. Hence, this first decade saw the Cadbury sugar division become leaner and more profitable. By 2000 it was ready to merge with the chocolate division under the banner Cadbury Trebor Bassett.

The Grocer magazine on Cadbury's rise

'The marriage of chocolate king Cadbury to sugar sovereign Trebor Bassett at the beginning of 2001 was one of the single biggest confectionery coalitions. By bringing Britain's favourite chocolate and sugar brands together, Cadbury Trebor Bassett positioned itself as the UK's leading confectionery company, holding pole position in both the chocolate and sugar sectors and grabbing an automatic 28% share of the £5.5 billion confectionery market comprising 70% chocolate and 30% sugar products.' The Grocer, 24th March 2001. Though this business coalition took place in 2001, Cadbury's dominance of the UK confectionery market was achieved in 1989 with its purchase of Trebor and Bassett.

Smaller product lines were simply not worth the marketing cost.

For that first decade following the sale, production continued in the main factories. Then in January 1999 Cadbury announced the closure of two plants over the next eighteen months: 300 jobs were to go at Maidstone, ending 119 years of sweet manufacture by the river there; this was a surprise as Cadbury had invested heavily in Maidstone during the mid 1990s to boost production of *Softmints*. Colchester, though a far more modern facility, was also due for the chop, along with 202 jobs. Production was to head north, some to Chesterfield, but most to Sheffield, Pontefract and York. The technical centre at Maidstone moved to Sheffield.

Then in 2003 the last remaining Trebor factory, at Chesterfield, was earmarked for closure. Cadbury announced that consumers no longer wanted the *Black Jacks* and *Fruit Salads* made there. 245 workers would lose their jobs. Admittedly, the Chesterfield plant was an ageing facility. But, just as at Maidstone and Colchester, the closure was a significant blow to the local population. By this point, fourteen years after the sale, Cadbury had closed every Trebor factory it had acquired.

A Trebor chewing gum

What would Sydney Marks have thought of it? In 2009, as part of one of the nation's largest confectionery launches, Cadbury introduced *Trebor Extra Strong Gum*.

Chewing gum offered scope for growth in the early twenty first century. UK consumers still chewed less gum than their counterparts in the US or elsewhere in Europe (while consuming above average amounts of other sweets). The gum market was then dominated by Chicago-based Wrigley, who did well to expand UK gum sales in the 1990s with its *Extra* and *Orbit* ranges. After purchasing Adams, Cadbury relaunched its *Trident* gum range in Britain in 2007.

As Trevor Bond, now President Markets for Kraft Foods Europe and then Cadbury MD for Britain and Ireland, recalls, 'Wrigleys thought we'd launch a mint gum through Trebor. Instead we launched a fruit and mint gum through Trident. Then as a second wave, we launched the Trebor gum, a plain mint gum, no-nonsense and cheaper than the Trident product.' In 2009 Cadbury launched *Trebor Extra Strong Gum* with a chunky £3.5 million advertising budget. The gum market was growing most among adults, who increasingly sought cleaner breath and a replacement for nicotine. Hence the freshness of mint as an avenue into gum, and hence this effort to harness the popularity of *Trebor Extra Strong Mints*, which still ruled the mint market. Ads for the new product stressed simply that Trebor now made a gum, while emphasising the mintiness of the Trebor brand.

Trevor Bond explains, 'British people see gum as minty, while foreigners see it as more things, such as fruity. Indeed, few other markets share the UK's love of strong mint. Continentals prefer lighter mints such as *Mentos*. We wanted to revolutionise the UK gum category – and we succeeded, gaining double digit category growth.'

But this wasn't Trebor's first gum. In 2003 the firm launched the ill-fated *Trebor 24-7* range of mints and gums, not just sugar-free but also promising to freshen breath and whiten teeth; the gums were called Mint Power Gum and Power Bright Gum. The so-called mouthfresh market was not impressed and the range was withdrawn the next year.

Below: from The Grocer magazine 15th August 2009: 'Cadbury has rested the gorilla, airport trucks and eyebrow-bouncing school kids in favour of a team of suited executives for its latest ad. The confectioner has invested £3.5m on the "Mint People" ATL campaign to support its new Trebor Extra Strong Gum, launched last month. It takes the form of a docu-soap, where an eager-to-please new recruit blurts out at a press conference that Trebor is launching a gum to the shock of his colleagues. With a "Sorry it took so long" strapline, the ad will run for four weeks from 24th August.'

Cadbury falls

Cadbury was also, by now, the world's largest confectionery business. It had recently spent $4.2 billion buying the US firm Adams, the world's second largest maker of chewing gum. To pay for this and other acquisitions, Cadbury laid off 5,500 workers and shut a fifth of its factories worldwide, aiming to save £400 million a year. Aside from Chesterfield, the other major closure in Britain was the Adams plant in Manchester which made Halls *Mentho-lyptus Lozenges*.

Cadbury may then have been the globe's biggest sweetmaker, but this size gave it little protection in a world increasingly dominated by hedge funds and other short term investors. In spring 2008 the Cadbury Schweppes group was broken up at the behest of a speculative billionaire who'd taken a 3% stake in the firm; the drinks arm of Schweppes was de-merged from the confectionery arm of Cadbury, even though the separation itself was expected to cost £1 billion, some 10% of the combined group's value. Shortly afterwards, Mars merged with Wrigley to become the world's top sweetmaker. Cadbury was now on its own, and no longer number one. But it was still a £10 billion company, with annual sales of £5 billion, a healthy business and one of the world's most respected brandnames. Surely that should be enough to survive?

It wasn't. Along came Kraft Foods, a food behemoth with annual sales of £26 billion but hungry for the growth prospects it saw in confectionery. Kraft's chairman Irene Rosenfeld made an aggressive bid for Cadbury, so instigating a bitter and very public takeover. Though the US firm promised safe stewardship of the new assets, critics pointed to its record with Terry, the York-based chocolate company which Kraft had repatriated to Eastern Europe in 2005. Once Kraft made the battle public, Cadbury's shares attracted the more opportunistic elements of the city, particularly hedge funds, who effectively pulled control of the firm's destiny away from Cadbury's board and older shareholders. By January 2010 the company had been sold. One week after purchase, Kraft announced the closure of the old Frys factory at Somerdale, which while bidding it had suggested it would maintain. Though Cadbury had already talked of closing the plant, a committee of British MPs said Kraft had acted 'irresponsibly and unwisely.'

Once Kraft made the battle public, Cadbury's shares attracted the more opportunistic elements of the city.

Yet it was British MPs who created the unregulated environment within which the sale took place. As Deborah Cadbury points out in her book *Chocolate Wars*, such an open-door policy for exposing British companies to foreign ownership would be unthinkable abroad. 'The Swiss have always protected Nestlé, allowing their food and chocolate industries to flourish.' She quotes Roger Carr, Cadbury chairman at the time of the sale, saying, 'In France, the loss of a "Cadbury" would have been out of the question. Germany believes that strength at home is the first stop to success abroad. In Japan, selling a company over the heads of management is unthinkable. And in the United States, regulations exist to protect strategic assets.'

Perhaps the best summary of the flawed system came from one of the stewards of that system: then secretary of state for business Peter Mandelson, who said, 'It is hard to ignore the fact that the fate of a company with a long history and many tens of thousands of employees was decided by people who had not owned the company a few weeks earlier and who had no intention of owning it a few weeks later.'

Stop Press

It's Kraft Foods no more. Just as this book went to press, news arrived that the 'global snacks powerhouse' was re-branding itself Mondelez. In calibrating the significance of this change, it's hard to improve on Mary Beth West, Executive Vice President and Chief Marketing Officer, who said: 'I'm thrilled with the name Mondelez International. It's interesting, unique and captures a big idea – just the way the snacks we make can take small moments in our lives and turn them into something bigger, brighter and more joyful.' Bill Hicks would have loved that.

The Trebor masterbrand

Farewell variety.

Once Cadbury bought the firm, there was no longer any need for Trebor factories, Trebor workers or Trebor managers. Everything functional became Cadbury (as later on everything at Bournville became Kraft). The word Trebor survived simply as a brand, a name for people to associate with products. But as the twentieth century came to a close, the nature of brands changed.

In the past, sweetmakers would present their products individually. *Refreshers* looked very different from *Extra Strong Mints*. *Dairy Milk* differed from *Milk Tray*. But as it became costly to advertise brands individually, marketers started getting excited about the notion of masterbrands – combining different products under one umbrella, and then focusing most advertising spend on that masterbrand. For Cadbury this meant giving all its chocolate products the same purple packaging and introducing us to a gorilla playing drums. Each product now pushed the purple Cadbury masterbrand. Not all separate lines fitted within this umbrella, so there was a radical rearrangement to focus on just a few. *Milk Tray*, for example, did not survive the cull. Sharps was severely demoted; together with other minor brands such as Pascalls, it was relaunched in 1999 within a new Bassett's Fundays range. 57 lines were reduced to 25. (In 2008 Cadbury sold the Sharp's brand, along with other names like Barratt, Jameson's and Butterkist, to Tangerine Confectionery, who today sell them as niche, nostalgic confections.)

But what of Trebor? Gradually all children's sweets were stripped from the brand, leaving mainly mints for adults. Bye-bye *Black Jacks*, farewell *Fruit Salad*, though those were to return under the Barratt name. In August 2001 Cadbury announced the creation of a Trebor masterbrand, comprising all products from the *Trebor Extra Strong Mints* and *Softmints* stables, including the 1999-launched *Trebor Mighty Mints,* plus two new products: *Trebor Menthol Vapour Mints* and *Trebor Mini Softmints*. Note how *Trebor* now becomes part of each product name.

Brand marketers do not like complex propositions, especially within the impulse purchase sector – those goods which people do not plan to purchase, but tend to buy on impulse when in the store. All Trebor products, and most Cadbury lines, fit within this sector. Chewing gum fits within an even tighter impulse sector: the Hot Zone, that small, warmly-contested area around the till where customers make their last minute decisions. They'll take a few steps for a chocolate bar, but not for gum, which must be within reach as they pay. To win attention within this tight, crowded space, it's vital the brands stand out. And to stand out, they must be simple. Hence Trebor's emergence as the mint brand. But not just any mint brand. Not fruity mint like *Trident*, or clinical mint like *Extra*, just a straightforward, 'charming' and 'passionate' mint product – that strives to be 'more than just a mint'. That's Trebor today.

As an official treat provider of the 2012 London Olympics, and unofficial ticket provider via customer competitions, Cadbury added logos for itself and the Games to the Trebor branding for the 'Baton of Sweet Success' promotion.

Even the word Trebor is less important than the colour scheme. Given the speed of impulse decisions, customers recognise the design of packaging faster than the writing, hence Cadbury's promotion of purple for chocolate. For *Trebor Extra Strong Mints*, this means the red star symbol in the centre of the packet containing the word Trebor. Indeed one could argue that all that once made Trebor proud – its plants, its products, its history, its name – has been replaced by a simple psychological association with a bright red star. Where once there was substance, now there is a shape.

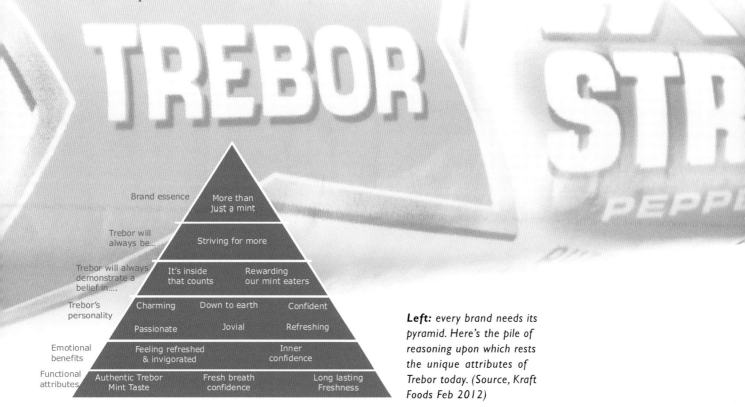

Brand essence	More than just a mint		
Trebor will always be...	Striving for more		
Trebor will always demonstrate a belief in....	It's inside that counts	Rewarding our mint eaters	
Trebor's personality	Charming	Down to earth	Confident
	Passionate	Jovial	Refreshing
Emotional benefits	Feeling refreshed & invigorated		Inner confidence
Functional attributes	Authentic Trebor Mint Taste	Fresh breath confidence	Long lasting Freshness

Left: *every brand needs its pyramid. Here's the pile of reasoning upon which rests the unique attributes of Trebor today. (Source, Kraft Foods Feb 2012)*

1936

The Robertson & Woodcock
List of Goods & Prices
for 10th August 1936

Super Boilings

8½d per lb
Almond Hardbake
Barley Sugar Super
Blackcurrant & Iodine
Cherry Coughs
Crystal Fruits
Crystal Mints
Dextro Butterscotch
French Almond Rock
Glycerine & Honey
Invalid Toffee
Menthol & Eucalyptus

8d per lb
Blackcurrant & Licorice
Chocolate Crispettes
Clear Fruit Fingers
Crystals Mints
Daddy Trebor Herbal Tablets
Devon Assorted
Extra Fine Acids
Fruit Centres
Imperial Acids
Imperial Fruits
Imperial Limes
Mentha-Euca
Milk Chocolate Bonbons
Old English Mints
Orchard Fruits
Orange & Lemon Barleys
Palace Mixture
Royal Acid Drops

7½d per lb
Acid Tablets Super
Aniseed Twist Super
Fruit Seals Super
Lemonade Bonbons
Paradise Fruits
Paregoric Tablets Super
Rose Refreshers
Sherbet Bonbons
Summer Refreshers

7d per lb
Brown Mint Crisp
Bullseyes
Grannies Chest Tablets
Lime Juice Nibs
West Indian Limes

6½d per lb
Acid Drops Super
Brandy Balls Super
Butter Slices
Clove Balls
French Almond Cubes
Mint Balls
Miracle Mints
Mothers Mints
Persian Sherbet
Raspberry Crystals

Special Packings:
Footballs
Mint Humbugs
Barley Sugar Sticks
Fancy Bottles
Barley Sugar Soldiers
Joyland Toffees
Xmas Rocks
Fudge Fancy Boxes

Creamy Toffee Tins:
Dick Whittington
Farmyard
Hesitation
Silver Sands

Trebor 1d Count Lines
Barley Fruit Sticks

Brompton Tablets
Cherry Barks
Chilnips
Crème de Menthe
Daytona Fruits
Doncaster Butterscotch
Extra Strong Peppermints
Ginger Beer
Koffades
Lemon Fizz
Lido Fruits
Orange & Lemon Drops
Orange Fizz
Royal Acids
Wine Drops
Buttermints
Full Cream Toffee
Lemonettes
Matador Mints
Sez You Toffee
Bobbies Choco Japs
Peter Pans
Harlequins
Choco Cubes
Black Boys
Bonny Boys
Carolinas
Doo Dahs
Lemonado
Lemonade Caramels
Lemon Cubes
Winter Cubes
Spearmint Cubes
Raspberry Cubes

Trebor ½d Count Lines
Army & Navy Tablets
Carnival Fruits
Clickety Clicks
Foaming Fizz
Fruity Chews
Herbal Tablets
Lemonade Cubes
Lemon Refreshers
Lushus Fruits
Parma Violets
Peerless Peppermints
Scented Bouquets
Sherbet Pops
West Indian Limes
Beatall Bars
Big Ben Bars
Bo'sun Bars
Buttermint Bars
Champ Toffee Bars
Cherry Cough Tablets
Crystal Bars
Egg & Milk Flaps
Fizz Whizz Bars
Flap Jacks
Football Flaps
Football Lollipops
Fruit Flans
Fruit Sundaes
Giant Black Jacks
Glider Bars
Golden Aero Bars
Humbug Bars
Icy Mints
Licorice Flaps
Lip Sticks
Lollibars
Long 'Uns
Luna Lollies
Natti-Paks
North Pole Tablets
Nuga Chocs
Raspberry Dab Suckers
Rugger Bars
Sambo Slices
Silver Fruit Tablets
Spearmint Bars
Speedway Bars
Super Spearminto
Toffee Crème Bars
Treacle Jacks
Watta Lollies
Winter Assorted

Assorted Pollylops
Bingo Bars
Chocolate Sonny Boys
Choco-Mac-Bars
Fruit Salad
God Star Bars
Jolly Boys
Monster Black Jacks
OK Fruit Bars
Orchard Fruits
Rainbow Mints
Empire Suckers
Sherbet Fountains

Trebor 1/4 d Count Lines
Chesties
Florals
Fruities
Fruit Monsters
Koffoes
Minties
Thirst Quenchers
Boat Race Chews
Black Jacks
Fruit Lumps Fruit Snaps
G.I.P.S.
I-Kan-Chews
Inky Dinks
Jazz Chews
Mint Bars
Rumba Bars
Snooker Snax
Sonny Boys
Winter Lumps
Choco Japs
Chocolate Nugo
Footer Chews
Grape Fruit Bricks
Ice Cream Bricks
Lemon Ice Bricks
Licorice Nugo
Pineapple Chews
Port Wine Chews
Rum & Butter Chews
Sports Chews
Umpties

Trebor Weight Lines
Dr Robertson's Nox-Kofs
Fizz-its
Lemon Fizz-its
Trebor Cherry Coughs
Trebor Mintoes
Chocolate Toffee Dainties
Fruit Chunks
Joyland Toffees
Cokernut Ice
Mint Gems
Trebor Herbals
Silver Crest Toffees
Sonny Boy Slab Toffee

Boleyn
Crunches, Cubes, Fingers
Butter Crunch
Buttermint Crunch
Fruit Crunch
Chocolate Crunch
Clear Mint Cubes
Egg & Milk Cubes
French Nut Cubes
Malt Cubes
Winter Cubes
Aniseed Fingers
Barley Fingers
Barley Butters
Barley Wafers
Butter Fingers
Clove Fingers
Greenland Mints
Eucalyptus Fingers
Iceland Mints
Malted Milk Fingers
Malted Scotch
Winter Fingers

Fruit Lines, Mixtures
Apricots

Ascot Fruits
Blackberries and Raspberries
Colonial Fruits
Empire Fruits
Festal Fruits
Fresh Fruits
Fruit Lollies
Grape Fruits
Icy Fruits
Mixed Fruit Fritters
Paradise Fruits
Tangerine Oranges
Texas Fruits
West Indian Limes
Aniseed Mixtures
Blackcurrant Mixture
Bunty Mixture
Butter Mixture
Chocolate Midgets
Dolly Mixture
Dorset Mixture
Duchess Mixture
Everybody's Mixture
Gala Mixture
Lemonade Mixture
Licorice Mixture
Midget Butters
Princess Mixture
Raspberry Mixture
Winter Mixture
Regatta Mixture

Pastilles, Rocks
Acid Pastilles
Buttermints
Chocolate Butters
Crème de Menthe Pastilles
Fruit Pastilles
Koff Kops
Cherry Cough Pastilles
Lemon Squash Pastilles
Lime Juice Pastilles
Mixed Pastilles
Orange and Lemon Pastilles
Boys and Girls Rock
Dolly Rock
Football Rock
French Nut Rock
Mint Sticks
Mixed Chocolate Rock
Orange and Lemon Rock
Rock Varieties

Satins, Bon Bons
Blackcurrant & Licorice Bonbons
Blackcurrant Satins
Chocolate Cracknels
Chocolate Cushions
Fairy Wands
Fruit Satins
Licorice Wafers
Malt Cracknels
Mint Cracknels
Peter Pans
Rose Satins
Rum & Butter Cracknels
Satin Cushions
Satinettes
Satin Jewels
Spearmint Wafers
Sweet Violets

Tubs, Fizzers
Brandy Kegs
Buttermint Tubs
Fizz Tubs
Fizz Wafers
Ice Cream Tubs
Lemon Fizzers
Lemon Tubs
Lemon Wafers
Mixed Fizzers
Orange Tubs
Raspberry Fizzers
Raspberry Tubs
Raspberry Wafers
Sherbet Bricks
Sherbet Fizzers

Sherbet Tubs
Sherbet Shells
Strawberry Ice Tubs
Treacle Tubs

Miscellaneous
Army & Navy Paregoric Tablets
Barley Sugar Twist
Best Fruit Balls
Bronchial Bricks
Butter Pats
Buttermint Humbugs
Cocoa Nibs
Chocolate Pods
Chocolate Wafers
Cokernut Brittle
Cokernut Toffee
Cough Twist
Dollies Bullseyes
Dollies Cloves-eyes
Sherbet Eyes
Fruit Bricks
Fog and Throat Tablets
Fruit Bricks
Fruit Twist
Glass Alleys
Glycerine and Lemon Drops
Golden Butter Balls
Harlequin Balls
Honey Bees
Honey Mints
Lime Bricks
Long Mints
Malted Mints
Mint Butters
North Pole Tablets
Orange and Lemon Quarters
Rum & Butter Pats
Spearmint Balls
Tangerine Balls
Voice Tablets
Winter Snaps

Balls
Acid Balls
Brandy Balls
Butter Balls
Cough Candy Balls
Golden Cough Candy Balls
Lime Balls
Ripe Goosberries
Winter Balls (Striped)
White Mint Balls

Bullseyes, Humbugs
Bristol Mints
Brown Bristol Mints
Brown Bullseyes
Bullseyes
Brown Clove Cushions
Brown Mint Cushions
Clove Eyes
Fruit Cushions
Kola Bon Bons
Mint Humbugs
Mint Tips
Mixed Mints
Winter Eyes

Drops, Seals, Tablets
Acid Drops
Aniseed Drops
Barley ABCs
Barley Fishes
Birds and Beasts
Blackcurrant Bars
Blackcurrant Ovals
Cats Tongues
Cherry Drops
Cherry Stones
Chocolate Teddies
Chocolate & Vanilla Tablets
Cockernut Bars
Cough Pips
Eucalyptus Tablets
Floral Tablets
Fruit Ovals,
Fruit Teddies

The shrinking product range

Take a look at these three lists of Trebor products. In 1936 there were 452 lines. By 1988 this had shrunk to 111. And today? Seven.

People still buy Trebor sweets. It's just they have far fewer different products to choose from. Back in the Thirties you could spend hours deciding between *Inky Dinks*, *Snooker Snax* or *Bo'sun Bars*. Much of this variety had gone by the Eighties, but even then you could find *Flutterbys*, *Woppa Chews* or *White Mice*. Now we're all too busy. We simply select gum or mints. Admittedly Trebor is now an adult brand, and a few of the old names still appear as niche products elsewhere. But back in the day, even adults had hundreds of sweets to consider.

Given the opportunity, most people would like more choice. Unfortunately, global food manufacturers have little interest in giving us that choice. It's much easier for them to produce a handful of lines and spend their money promoting the overall brand. Yes, it's gospel that the convenience of modern corporation-driven capitalism gives us a better life. But let your mind wander through these names of sweets from the Thirties. Think of the people who made them and the people who ate them – and ask yourself whether buying and eating sweets in those days wasn't perhaps, in some ways, a bit more fun.

Fruit Wafers
Herbal Bars
Lemon, Lime & Acids
Lime Bars
Lime Nibs (green)
Lime Nibs (white)
Midglet M & E Tablets
Montpelier Drops
Orange and Lemon Slices
Orange Pips
Oriental Fruits
Paradise Plums
Pears, Large
Phizoggs
Pineapple Drops
Small Fishes
Sonny Boy Drops
Tiny Cough Tablets
Tiny Fruits
Winter Warmers

Mixtures
Carnival Mixture
Little Folk Mixture
Jazz Mixture
Rugby Mixture
San Toy Mixture
Toffee Mixture

Rocks
Broken Butterscotch
Brown Mint Rock
Fruit Rock

Jam Roll
Raspberry Rock
Rhubarb Custard
Rock Allsorts
Sherbet Rock
Summer Rock

Toffees, Rings
Devon Toffee
Old English Toffee
Cokernut Rings
Cough Rings
Fairy Rings
Spearmint Rings

Boleyn Lemonade Powder
Boleyn Raspberry Crystals
Boleyn Grape Fruit Powder
Boleyn Sherbet
Empire Cocktails

Odd Weights
Mint Sticks
Icy Fruits
Mint Cracknels
Sherbet Bricks
Sherbet Shells
Tangerine Quarters
Fizz Wafers
Raspberry Wafers
Cats Tongues
Cokernut Rings
Fruit Wafers

1988

The Trebor Limited Retail Price List for 8th August 1988

ROLLS
Mints
Extra Strong Mints – King Size
Softmints/Softmints Spearmint
Mint Imperials
Spearmint Imperials
Coolmints
Trebor Mints
Trebor Spearmints

Fruits
Softfruits
Refreshers
Trebor Wine Gums Large
Trebor Wine Gums Small
Tropical Pastilles
American Hard Gums Large
American Hard Gums Small
Fruit Pastilles

Others
Milk Gums
Cherry Drops
Aniseed Imperials

WEIGH-OUT
Boxes
Trebor Wine Gums
American Hard Gums
Milk Gums
Mini Wine Gums
Salad Gums
Midget Gems
Jelly Babies
Mint Imperials
Jelly Beans
Mint Creams

Jars
Kola Kubes
Sherbet Lemons
Strawberry Sherbets
Kopp Kopps
Cough Candy Twist
Pear Drops
Pineapple Chunks
Toffee Crunch
Blackcurrant Aniseed Sherbets
Buttermints
Crystals
Frosties
Everybody's Mixture
Extra Strong Mints
Toffee Bon Bons
Strawberry Bon Bons
Lemon Bon Bons
Fruit Salad
Mint Imperials

Great Spearmint Imperials
Aniseed Imperials
Pancho Raisins
Pancho Peanuts
Assorted Toffee, Top Cream
Dairy Fudge
Iced Caramels
Choc Eclairs
Softmints
Softmints Spearmints
Softfruits

CHILDRENS
Sugar Coated Mallows
Fruit Salad
Black Jack
Woppa Chew Cola/Spearmint
Postman Pat
Apple Chew
Flutterbys Chocolate
Flutterbys Caribbean
Penny Pets
Penny Coins
White Mice
Little Big Feet
Trebor Hands
Jelly Rings
Gum Fruits
Trendy Trainers
Wrigglers
Kola Bears
Cobblestones
Glitter Grubs
Kool Kola Katz
Jelly Animals
Postman Pat
My Little Pony
Milk Teeth
Great Munchy Mushrooms
Bubble Gum Fruits
Assorted Tools
Fish 'n' Chips
Postman Pat
My Little Pony
Transformers
Fudgy Bars
Toffee Lolly
Beatall Lolly
Fizzy Kola Lolly
Dinosaur '5's
Record Breakers '5's
Space '5's
Nutto Chew Bar
Cola Refreshers
Big Chuckles
Kola Frosties
Fruit Flavour Frosties
Pineapple Frosties
Black Jack Stickpack
Fruit Salad Stickpack
Lollyade, Mix of Lollydips
Canadian Apples

BAGS
All as above

BARS
Chocolate Coconut Ice
Soft Nougat Small
Soft Nougat Large
Soft Nougat Giant
Chocolate Soft Nougat

2012

Kraft Foods, 18th Feb 2012
Trebor Extra Strong Mint Spearmint
Trebor Extra Strong Mint Peppermint
Trebor Softmints Spearmint
Trebor Softmints Peppermint
Trebor Softfruits
Trebor Extra Strong Gum Spearmint
Trebor Extra Strong Gum Peppermint

Trebor today

Trebor survives as a name, as one of Kraft's masterbrands. So long as consumers continue to want *Extra Strong Mints*, the name Trebor will survive. But should that desire wane, the name will fade with it. No longer does the word Trebor stand for any people, places or notions beyond profit. Trebor, today, is simply a marketing formula, marshalled by a brand team.

Marketing priorities are nothing new in sweets. Firms like Cadbury and Trebor long traded on deft manipulation of consumer emotions. But this was never all that they did. It's fair to say that many of the people who bought a bar of *Dairy Milk* back in the 1930s might have had some sense of the company behind that product; the factory at Bournville or the Quaker spirit of the owners. Some firms, such as Terry's of York, even put their hometown into their name. Today, however, brands hold little of substance. They have become artificial constructs, engineered to appeal in the same way chemical flavourings are used to make potato crisps taste like prawns or roast beef.

The Marks family had a powerful sense of loyalty to people and place.

Modern corporations are similarly artificial constructs, configured around the needs of their market, with little loyalty to anything but the needs of that market. Indeed, they eagerly sever any ties to remain as 'mobile', 'flexible' and 'responsive' as possible. It's instructive to compare such attitudes to those of business dynasties such as the Marks or Cadbury families. The Marks were, admittedly, quite capable of closing a factory, as they did with the large Clarnico works in 1969 soon after they bought it (though few could have made a serious business case to keep that works alive); and Cadbury, in the end, closed all the Trebor plants. But the Marks had a powerful sense of loyalty to people and place. Their new Colchester plant did not feature night shifts because the directors, ignoring the scorn of some business advisers, felt such practices were inimical to family life. Workers from the Forest Gate factory remember Ian Marks' tears when announcing its closure. And when the family sold the business, it chose to give – unprompted – tens of millions of pounds to those who had worked for the firm. Can you imagine the shareholders of any modern corporation allowing its directors to display such principle or generosity?

Admittedly Sydney Marks did not care for trades unions. But his dislike stemmed not from the demands that unions make. He just didn't want anyone standing between him and his workers who were, to him, like family. Indeed he expected Trebor staff to enjoy better conditions than in unionised factories.

One might argue such paternalism was like the better sort of colonialism; it treated the natives decently, but didn't give them the vote. But at least it treated them well. And given the powerlessness of most workers within the flexible, global markets of today, there is something to be said for a time when jobs typically lasted for decades.

No system is perfect. No boss can expect to be loved. But time and again Trebor went further than it needed to look after its staff. And many of those staff, just like the Marks family, felt intense loyalty to the place they worked. Cadbury's Quaker tradition couched this in more overtly spiritual terms, but the essential attitude was the same: that ownership confers responsibility. It is not simply a financial relationship.

Looking back, Trebor was an extremely successful business. From the hundreds, maybe thousands, of tiny enterprises boiling sugar at the start of the twentieth century, this East End partnership pulled ahead of the rest to become the nation's largest sugar confectioner. Its name sat happily in generations of memory banks. It delighted kids and grown ups with novel, delicious treats. It provided reliable employment for many families of workers. It built factories in poor countries more used to being exploited for their resources. It was acclaimed for export within a country famous for trading. It pioneered more humane ways of organising work. And when the company passed on, it did so with dignity.

Number one in mints: *as of February 2012, Trebor was the UK's largest mint brand with 40% of the market. The Softmints range alone represented half of Trebor's £56.7m annual sales, while Extra Strong Peppermint was the best selling single mint product. (Figures Nielsen 18.02.12)*

Index

Matthew Crampton lives in London. He has long worked as a writer and is related to the Marks family who owned Trebor.

Thanks

I am grateful to the Marks for supporting this book, particularly to John, Ian, Wenna and Angela Marks for their contribution to its content and to Chris Marks for co-ordinating the family involvement. For some personal memories of Trebor I drew on interviews within the Trebor Archive undertaken by Nottingham University Business School. Charles Woodhouse provided insight as the one-time Trebor lawyer and long-term advisor to the Marks family. Clive Robertson shared with me his history of the Robertson family; sadly he died while this book was being written.

I owe particular thanks to Sarah Foden and Jackie Jones from the Cadbury Archive (now Kraft Foods UK Archives) at Bournville in Birmingham. They are custodians of the Trebor materials and have been wonderfully helpful at all stages of creating this book. Thanks also to Sandy Brand, Keith Newton, Trevor Bond, Tony Bilsborough, Emily Woodward-Smith and Gary Carcary from Kraft Foods for answering my questions.

I recommend Nicholas Whittaker's book *Sweet Talk – The Secret History of Confectionery* and thank him for giving permission to include some extracts from it. Deborah Cadbury's *Chocolate Wars* is another good read.

I spent happy hours with the team who used to work at Newham Council Archives – Kathy Taylor, Brian Fitzsimons, Paul Pert and Bill Durie – and thank them for their remarkable help and knowledge of East London history. Thanks also to Rachel Deeson at Bygone Kent, Cliff Lea & Philip Cousins of NEDIAS (North East Derbyshire Industrial Archaeology Society), Sarita Bhatia and Kimberley Richardson at the Olympic Park Legacy Company, Anne-Marie Knowles of Chesterfield Borough Council, Val Carman and Professor Ronald Brech. Adam Brown and Steve Kamlish advised on design and Ivor Kamlish helped with the map of East London. Henry Ling are patient printers and their prepress manager Iain Robinson was a steady guide to my attempts at learning book production.

Rise again

This is an artist's impression of the Olympic Park that hopes to arise in East London once the 2012 Games are over. Around the stately debris of the stadia should appear five new neighbourhoods, one of which – Sweetwater – is named after the confectionery industry which once thrived there. Sweetwater sits upon the spot A where in 1907 thousands of staff crafted sweets at the grand old firm of Clarnico.

At the same time over a century ago, two miles away in Forest Gate B, Messrs Robertson, Woodcock, King and Marks set up their tiny sugar-boiling venture. Each had come from the tough old East End C to start afresh in the new East End across the River Lee D. These sweet firms depended on the Henry Tate sugar refinery E, the London docks F and the fast expanding population of new boroughs like East Ham, Plaistow, West Ham and Forest Gate (across the centre left of the picture).

Sixty two years later in 1969, with a grand firm of their own, Messrs Marks and Robertson were able to buy Clarnico for Trebor Sharps. Gradually they moved production out to the suburbs and elsewhere, closing first the Clarnico plant then later the original factory in Forest Gate. Gradually this area around the River Lee returned to its marshy origins, a rare rural retreat within the city. Now, tamed by the Olympic Park, it's set to rise once again.

Image looks south from a point just north west of Stratford. See also map on Page 11. Image copyright of Olympic Park Legacy Company 2011.